ALONE: IN THE WORLD: LOOKING

Elroy Bode

ALONE
IN THE WORLD
LOOKING

by

ELROY BODE

TEXAS WESTERN PRESS

———◆◆◆———

THE UNIVERSITY OF TEXAS AT EL PASO

© 1973

TEXAS WESTERN PRESS

THE UNIVERSITY OF TEXAS AT EL PASO

Library of Congress Catalog Card 73-76995

ISBN 0-87404-046-9

Illustrations by

ANTONIO PADILLA PIÑA

PROLOGUE

WHEN I LEFT THE FAMILIAR structures of home at seventeen and went off to college, it was as if I had walked flat-footed and casually whistling into a brick wall called life. I spent the next twenty years or so trying to recover from the impact.

I was stunned by the knowledge that I was alive on the earth and didn't know what to do about it; it was as though I had been reborn, wide-eyed and vulnerable, into a world of gigantic, hidden meanings. Others seemed to know, almost serenely, what they ought to be doing; I did not. I was haunted by memories, and almost paralyzed by the awesome shapes of reality. What was the purpose of my life, I wanted to know — the purpose of anything, for that matter?

As I walked though the days, as years passed, I kept trying to find satisfying answers to the questions that plagued me. I wanted values I could believe in, and I thought that if I looked hard enough, long enough, I would find them. I was on a quest — a private, intense search for truth, for God, for myself — and I was determined to discover, or perhaps create, some kind of order out of the chaos around me.

The pages that follow represent part of that single-minded attempt to make sense of the world. They are also a record of my concern with the written word — the power, the lure, the mystery of writing. For as I looked and reflected and waited — seeing here a sad man's face, feeling there a pleasant creek breeze — I wanted to do the impossible: to lift life out of itself and make it live a second time on my pages. The desperate urge to explore life gradually became, therefore, a desperate urge to tell about it. As I typed and retyped my conversations with myself — in San Antonio, on the Gulf Coast, in the hill country, in Dallas, in El Paso — I guess I secretly hoped that the scenes, thoughts, observations, sketches I was writing down might some day form the mosaic of that Absolute I was so doggedly seeking. Of course this was not the case. Yet such a journal did serve to record the only adventure I have ever had: the attempt to know the depths of myself and my surroundings.

I

1954 - 1961

I

WHY THE CONTINUOUS beginnings of life? Why do eons pass like colored slides in a projector, and history seem no more than a spilled pile of typewriter ribbon on which words were written. Why keep having these individual exercises in Lifemanship; why always the infinite perfection of *one more*. Why one more piece of throbbing conscience, one more set of eyes. Why one more of her, the little girl in the drive-in laundry: why another starched blue dress and black patent shoes and white socks neatly turned down one turn. Why another unsuspecting, unknowing, innocent face. (Instead of smiling at her, I should have yelled: It's too late now; you're already in for it. You're alive now and you've got to go ahead. But that starched dress and that candy bar you're setting so much store by now — they won't be of much use to you. Try them for a while, but you'll see.)

Why the continual lighting of fires, why the brief glows and quivers of flame that reach up and attain one concentrated point and for a moment seem to beg for just one worthy object to consume, or at least scorch; why the gradual disappointed sagging down of the flames upon themselves, why the gradual growing into yellowness and sputtering and a final dying out, why another small patch of white ashes on an already ash-covered ground.

I AM, EVIDENTLY, an anti-evolutionist in one sense: I dislike not the belief that today's life was produced from lesser forms but the notion that those living in the distant past lived less of life than we do now. I don't like the idea of there having been expendable pawns in life, of some people being used up in the slow perfectability of an elite group. I object to the idea that God, through a superbly developed slow-motion technique, is gradually revealing His wonders and truths and self across the ages, with everyone along the way helping to pave the road for the future race of Perfected Men. I don't mind not being among the boys at the finish line, nor do I mind being in the same boat, evolutionally speaking, with brown sea algae and Alley Oop. I just don't like being expendable.

I REMAIN DISTURBED, like a self-conscious oyster, wondering if my continual inner tension might someday mean a pearl.

NOTE TO A DEAD LIEUTENANT: Your room down the hall is empty, George Murdock; you are dead at 25. You died like a novice — wearing blue cotton pajamas and carrying a tube of Ipana toothpaste in your hand.

At a time when young service men can at least die in spectacular, if not always heroic, ways, you went far too routinely. We are left only with a report that nature failed you, stopped supporting your heart. There is no grim tale, just a silent room and cotton pajamas.

What a thin memory we have of you — merely that of a rather private young man who lived out his life sensibly and without blemish. Quietly you lived and quietly you died: how easy a summary. . . .

It does not seem right, somehow, to let you go with just incredulous tones of disbelief. We should raise lumps in our throats, give you a decent show of sorrow. But because we did not know you well, barely recognized you as a face and a name, we will simply feel awed for a while and then forget you — following that curious law of the heart that tells us we cannot spend our grief on those we have not intimately known.

We who are left will fight many battles of the soul, gain comforts, seek truth, meet defeats — come to know the full curve of life, perhaps, before we are through. You departed the race with the sound of the starting gun still ringing in your ears.

IF ONLY I could get the riverbanks or the trees or the soil to talk, *then* maybe I would know something.

LATE AT NIGHT I catch my lips sneaking out their old call letters: GOD. I catch them fumbling automatically to shape that desperate signal they've been giving out for the past few years: that shameless burlesque and paraphrase of SOS.

THERE IS ONLY one way in which I can ever be at peace with myself — to be convinced that I have within me a steady source of significant things to say about life and have the ability to write them down so that others will value them. If I were Jesus Christ and Abe Lincoln rolled into one, I would nevertheless carry within me a sense of failure if I did not write because to create memorable things out of my head is the only challenge I accept. I must be able to look at the world, perceive true things about it, and write them down — or fail. (Each day for the past couple of years I have risen to the world like a blind trout to the surface of a creek; but, being blind, I see no big truths to snap at. I only sense they are there, and desire to have them. And so each day, unsatisfied as a trout without his bug, I slide back to the depths. I will rise again tomorrow, though, and the next day. . . .)

WRITING, FOR ME, is an expression of a truth deeply felt and joyously perceived.

GRASS, GROWING ALONE in some off-place — how long it has been since I last, with something like real gladness, reached down from my concerns and noticed it, still green, almost polite-looking, remarkably constant and unperturbed.

SOMETIMES IT SEEMS that I don't know anything anymore. I seem bankrupt of every bit of certainty I ever possessed.

SCENE ON SUNDAY MORNING: a pinch-faced blond girl of

13 in a purple Boy Scout shirt with a scab on her chin slowly feeding sawdust off a pier to a school of mullet. She looks as if she would just as soon date a mullet as not, or have intercourse with it. She herself already a cold fish, a-moral, a-something. Would marry a Martian.

SOMETIMES I PULL GOD out of a box, dust Him off, wind Him up, set Him in place on a pedestal, and then expect Him to go to work.

YOU'VE GOT TO LICK time first. You must break the long habit of thinking that the common unit of measure is the hour, or the day. Time must not hold a whip. Its steady passing must not upset you too much.

Thinking either of it or of what your contemporaries are accomplishing puts you into a competitive frame of mind — something you must never allow, if you ever want to do anything good.

SOMETIMES WHEN I THINK something "significant" in my mind, I find that I force myself to say it outloud — as if the thought, unvocalized, would not be recognized and IBM-ed by the Great Invisible Recorder.

IT WAS FRIDAY AFTERNOON and I was just driving around in my green Ford, sipping a beer, feeling the cool air through my window, enjoying the post oaks that broke the sunlight into long, end-of-the-day splotches.

I felt free and relaxed — even as the road signs announced "SLOW CAMP BULLIS 15 M.P.H." Dutifully, I slowed my speed and eased into the outskirts. I was not on duty, I was not in uniform, I had no connection with this depressing collection of leftover buildings from World War II. I was merely a citizen in a car, driving patiently past trucks and jeeps and clipped, faded grass and big squares of abandoned concrete foundations. Camp Bullis was just a half-abandoned little army post in tick-and-cedar country, driven through and forgotten in a minute.

Yet just that minute was enough for a sense of bleakness to overwhelm me. The grounds looked deserted, empty. Even the grass was not pleasant to look at because it was tainted — ruined by being *military grass*. But it was the building that depressed me: a long yellow wooden building, its paint faded, sitting off in a little low place near a clump of oaks. At five-thirty the sun was plastered across its side. During the brief time of my looking it seemed — that wall, that barracks, that low place beside the oaks — to be the loneliest possible place on earth. I imagined a man in khakis — forced to remain on base over the weekend to perform some routine, useless duty — as he walked back to the barracks in the Friday afternoon sun. I could see him opening the barracks door and going inside — listening to the sound of his army shoes echoing across the floor. I could see him as he walked into the warm airless latrine and stared into the small mirror hanging on a gray latrine wall. And as he listened to the sparrows making their many afternoon sounds in the oak trees outside the window, I could see him take out his razor and slit his throat while the gnats swarmed in the air and the sun continued to flood against the west barracks wall and the military trucks stood with their tires in a row against the yellow lines of the motor pool lot.

I LOOK FOR A WAY to act, to think, to begin a life's work. I fear that I have no original stuff, that I will always be weighing, considering, reading, watching, wondering — never sure. Therefore I go around treading lightly and keeping a good look out, as if I am some Saul of Tarsus watching for my own Damascus Road.

MOST PEOPLE WOULD SAY that the proper cure for egocentricity is to get out of yourself — give yourself to others.

But there is wrong in this. "You lose yourself in the giving," they say. That's true. And that's the wrong in it. It is merely nerve-steadying escapism. You cross yourself off in order to concentrate on others.

The cure for self-centeredness is not to lose but to find your-self — to make a gift of yourself to yourself. You must discover yourself and be content. This way you win; the other way you merely forfeit.

THE DEMANDS ON A PERSON — the demands of his reason, the demands of his hopes, the demands of his emotions, the demands of his vanity, the demands of his conscience, the demands of his understandings, the demands of his failures, the demands of his weaknesses, the demands of his strengths. How does a person ever really function? He's all conflict.

JUST DON'T FORGET THIS: that you must never write about things you don't *care* about. Don't try to be Capable, writing about anything and everything. A person simply doesn't care about anything and everything. He cares selectively; he has primary areas of concern and he should work solely within them. Remain, first and always, a human being. Have the cares of a human being, not a writer. Remain the *you* that you were before you ever heard of writers and writing. Remember that you would never have writ-ten a line in the first place if you had not *cared* enough about something to want to tell about it (you just didn't sit down to exercise a talent). Continue to do this — to write only out of care, concern, passion.

WHY DOES EVERYONE, in order to be mentally healthy, have to superimpose some other name upon himself and be called Plumber or Doctor or Teacher? Why is it that just calling your-self what you are — a human being — is not identification enough, even to yourself?

THE SENSUALITY of small brown birds flying straight into

the heart of bare willow trees along a river: joining the leafless spacious limbs in one abrupt, quiet fusion.

I SIT IN MY CAR on Sunday afternoon beside a plowed field, writing a little about isolated things: the beauty of a tree shadow; the sound of a dog barking as a group of children run unseen through distant trees; the smell of grass and flowers and fresh dirt that a breeze brings to you; the steady heavy-sweet smell of acres of mesquites in bloom; a few bobbing-necked doves eating hurriedly, suspiciously along the railroad track; a bird — far out in the mesquites and hidden — that makes a quick, incessant sound that is useless to describe unless you have heard it once on a hot, quiet afternoon in South Texas.

And with the air smelling the way it does, and with the dark plowed field stretched out in the low sun the way it is, and with unseen running dogs and children, and gradually shadowing grass, and a light continual breeze, and night coming out of nowhere like a slow ground mist — you feel you must put something down. It won't be much, but you feel you must pay homage to the day.

THERE IS THAT TIME when you realize that good things can be gone forever. Your reaction to this blunt fact is the first great testing ground.

I WONDER IF ONCE this sac is drained within me, will it fill up again? Is the desire in me concentrated, like the aching pus from a single sore? And once punctured — and the pressure relieved — will the pressure build up again? Does my pressure come from that "one book" or is it a steady force, a geyser?

THIS AFTERNOON I watched a man fishing at the bay. He was a big, one-armed man in a white T-shirt and baseball cap who stood at the end of the pier with his son and cast out into the water with long tireless loops from his surf rod. His son sat on an up-ended bucket, using a small cane pole. They fished there most of the afternoon without ever showing either enthusiasm or boredom. They did not have any luck, but if they had caught some fish I'm sure the fish would have reflected the man's lack of emotion: they would have got aboard the hooks with the professional disinterest and air of routine that brakemen use in getting aboard trains: just meeting their conveyor and being borne away. . . .

When the sun was nearly down the man stuck the butt end of his surf rod under the stump of his left arm and reeled in one last slow time with his good arm and then turned and began to lumber in from the end of the long pier. The boy shouldered his pole and walked along behind his father, carrying his bucket. There was no more fuss to their walking than there had been to their fishing. When they reached their car at the baithouse they disappeared into it and the man steered it evenly and continuously out of sight down the beach toward the road to town. Their passing from view was so effortless, so casual and yet so complete, that it was almost dreamlike: I felt that if I had idled over to where the car had driven away in the sand, I would have found no tracks.

ON POETRY, *and the one who would attempt to write it: Poetry emerges from loneliness and a sense of space. To be "poetically aware" is to be physically aware: to suddenly perceive your physical surroundings in terms of innumerable harmonious corridors of sight and sound, all of which seem to be passing straight through you effortlessly (—how much does this relate to childhood, when actual doors were always opening and shutting in the late afternoon and when there was usually a hallway tunneling its way somewhere through the house? how much, for me, is this a carry-over from those long five-and-six o'clock odysseys in and out of doors and trees and gates; those times I spent idling away myself and the afternoon?)*

a child's voice floats by itself somewhere, and you hear it; a black dog trots along a still-damp sidewalk, and you see him; shadows slant outward from buildings, and you walk through them: all these events, so very small and uncomplicated and common, are the things of which poetry is made. Poetry is just human reaction to the simple riches of the physical world.

suddenly, when there is peace enough, and time enough, and space enough — and when your body and its senses are aware enough — you are finally ready to receive it: that moment of sustained awareness.

yet, strangely enough, you come closest to accepting death at the moment you are most intensely, poetically, aware of life. For having so completely suffused yourself in the pulsing world, you nearly lose the sense of your own identity (—a curious thing: that the poetic impulse, even as it makes you stretch out to the beauties of existence, tends toward anti-life: even as it makes you passionate for life it attempts to transcend life, to penetrate it — and by its own intense trajectory, to go beyond it).

SOUTH FLORES STREET: it dips unevenly through the heart of South San Antonio on its way out of town. In some of the dips clumps of pecan trees grow beside small drive-in grocery stores, and sweating Mexican men stand in the shade of the trees drinking red soda water and Pearl beer.

It is August, and Mexican people are sweating all over the South Side.

In front of the Ortega Brothers Garage a short fat woman wheels a baby carriage along, with two open-mouthed, heat-sleeping babies sweating inside it. Three barefooted girls follow the woman as she pushes the squeaking carriage down the sidewalk. The sun touches them hard.

A man picks his teeth as he sits on his front porch, barefooted, in his undershirt, looking out.

In the distance trees swim in the sunlight.

I THINK I HAVE BEEN, without knowing it, trying to give life to things which have no voices. It is as though I want my words to set free the things which, without a voice, would have no meaning. It is as if I am saying to myself: There is beauty locked in many places; people will not find it unless you lend them your eyes and let them see.

(. . . As yet, no one has ever put *afternoon* into words.)

Perhaps this is it: One must not try to describe something, not tell *about* it, but with the right words let the thing itself come to life. Through your words let it find its tongue. Let it rise out of muteness and let it speak in its own syllables. You must not use your own. Let the thing speak for itself and stand in its own beauty. Let the afternoon tell you about itself. Let it find its own rhythm.

I LOOK AT A FLY and think: How does that little son of a bitch get around? But he does. And the way he suddenly takes off and goes somewhere, you can rest assured he knows more about his business in this world than I do about mine.

YOU CAN NEVER turn your back on God and be left with any reason for life. Yet you try to keep your face toward Him and you never see a damn thing.

FIRST SHADOWS: How hard it is not to see everything through the eyes of childhood. . . .

Take a look out your window some fall morning when the leaves of an elm tree are shadowed and waving against the grass. Isn't the emotion which you feel the same as that which you felt years ago — when, inches high above the ground, you wandered among the sights and smells of life for the first time? Can splotched shadows on bright morning grass ever have any meaning different from the one which causes you to say, now, to the window: My God, they have never changed. . . . I am looking straight into the heart of something which I knew intimately but which has become so much a part of me I can't even remember what it is anymore.

Shadows of leaves against bright October ground: Could such things be what an adult would notice on his own, spontaneously? Possibly not. But a child, in his newness: he looks about him with an open, ready eye and is pleased. He allows shadows — out of the pleasure and sense of mystery they give — to pierce his body like germs seeking their host.

The body, the eye of a child: Will we ever escape from what it felt and saw? Our impressive layers of adult flesh tend to hide, to deny, that previous small person. Yet they cannot. They merely serve to deepen that tunnel down which we look as we gaze toward the source of our earliest, and perhaps greatest, light.

I WANT THE POWER to translate to other people, through words, the things that tear me apart each day.

NIGHT FISHING on the coast: It was only Mitch and I who wanted to continue fishing at night. He would light his after-supper cigar — first puffing on it a little to be sure it was caught — and then after gathering up the rods and stringers and metal fishing boxes we had laid down beside the tent, we would leave the others and walk the hundred yards or so up the beach to the pier.

The wind would be blowing in strong from the Gulf and the waters would seem magically wide and black as we walked toward the end of the pier. We would find a place underneath one of the small high bulbs and put down our gear and begin to cast out into the darkness. And as I fished — the wind in my face, the surf breaking easily along the shore — it always seemed to me that there was a quiet fraternity among those who had scattered out along the railings. Everyone stood there patiently — casting, waiting, looking at the bay and the stars and the night — and no one seemed to care, really, if he caught anything or not. People seemed content just to stand there and let the waters lap against the dark pilings underneath and the Gulf wind blow steadily across their bodies.

It seems impossible that anyone on that peaceful stretch of

boards should have ever found a reason to become angry: it was as though human emotions were completely diluted — were in solution with the night and the Gulf and the sweeping salt air. . . . Perhaps a fishing pier is the one place on earth where a war could never start — where no one would take aggression seriously.

LITERARY TYPES: they know how to make the proper adjectives out of writers' names. How they love to hear themselves say: Chekovian, Faulknerian, Dickensian.

SUNDAY AT FOUR, when the precise touch of the unknowable universe is upon human sensibilities.

AN AVERAGE WOMAN'S MAN is synonymous with strength and endurance and courage. If life hurts this man, he must not show it. He must be able to absorb all that life can throw his way and still keep going. If it becomes necessary — to preserve order in life, perhaps — that he inflict pain, he must inflict it. Or if it is even necessary that he kill in the line of some duty, then he must be capable of doing that and not think excessively about it. He must always be the one who keeps going. He must not have the luxury of showing despair.

An average woman's man must want his woman and be kind to her, but he must be able to leave her at any time, if some circumstance demands it. He must never be wholly committed to her but, instead, to his work. And she must know this.

He must never ask openly for strength or fortitude.

He does not have to be wholly admirable but, instead, respected.

The woman first respects him, then loves him — with part of the love coming out of the respect (which can be partly based on fear). She must never feel pity for her man, or else she will, at some crucial point, straighten out his tie for him and pat his shoulder and leave him sorrowful at the station. The woman does not want a friend or a companion; she wants a man, a husband, who can perhaps be these other things secondarily. (The woman will not grant a friend his faults but she will a man. She will not only grant them but will try to adjust to them.)

The man need not possess wisdom or romance; the woman will try to find these as she can. It is only necessary that when the two of them walk down the street, the man's head must be straight and to the front. It will be the woman's head that is turned to his.

No other combination will last, I am sorry to say.

I GO ABOUT, penning my stray lambs of thought like an indulgent shepherd. I don't suppose I will ever stock an XIT ranch with them. Rather, I will just go about the countryside, gathering here and there, never driving them to market, just letting them graze in my private lots: a dilettante's flock.

SOMETIMES I THINK sex and books will send me to near madness.

I SCRAPE SMALL sure words off my brain — fragments. Nothing big seems to be going on within me.

THERE HAVE ALWAYS been great people, wholly sincere, who have looked at the same object and called it different names and have been ready to fight for the validity of their own descriptions. Thus it seems that such a term or ideal as "an open mind" — the free mind, the mind nearest to that of a terribly judicious God — can never be used when talking about the human mind, for it can never be open or free. The human mind is like a roller coaster car on the roller coaster track. The car, regardless of the heights it climbs, the intricate turns it makes, always travels at the courtesy of the track laid for its purposes. Some people have small, uninteresting tracks, very nearly on a plateau, with but a few minor dips and curves; others have tracks that extend in every way, with breath-taking swoops and curves. But always the cars — the thoughts, the ideas — remain the guests of the tracks. They can go fast, travel apparently with wills of their own, but are always captive agents, sufficient to themselves only when aloft on those well-laid, indispensable tracks.

A THIN-NECKED WOMAN sits by herself in the San Antonio train station. She seldom makes any kind of movement but when she does it is to put her hand to her cheek and touch a skin irritation there.

She is an alone little woman, prepared to travel.

Her tweed coat hangs neatly over the back of the bench, and one end of her small brown suitcase is set squarely against the seat. Train time is still an hour away but she holds her ticket and her purse tightly in her lap — as if they are all she has now to ward off the vague and persistent fears of increasing old age.

I HAVE NO REAL INTELLIGENCE; my mind is merely attentive to the findings of my body.

I CAN NEVER quite forget *the greater context of our lives* — that great unknown which makes a mockery of our intense human concerns.

HOW DOES A PERSON go about making any kind of peace with himself if he knows that what he wants is not a moment for the space of a moment but that moment *for keeps?* Let's say you find something nice, as we always do: for a while time is suspended for you, and life and the earth are split open before you like the two fine-smelling halves of an apple. But then time suddenly awakens and yawns and slaps your good moment with the back of its hand, and the moment quickly passes on, chastened.

. . . Even books — they take on this same quicksilver quality. For what can a book really do for you? You're in it, you're nodding your head yes; you're breathing in the lives and overhearing the thoughts and getting a little dry-mouthed sometimes from the power of the author's vision — and then, the book is over. You close it and it is a part of you and yet it, too, is to be all memory. You eat up 500 pages of a man's mind and bam! you are finished with *him.* Next!

I WONDER if I have, really, any other drive that can touch the drive to love, to lavish love, to pour love out of me, to let love seep and flow over the person or thing and then to sit and hold it in the center of my body.

SOLITARY OAKS, like huge tarantulas camouflaged in green.

WRITING SINCE high school has been largely compulsive. I have tried to take advantage of the things I have done and observed by writing about them, rationalizing that all my non-productive, un-scholarly hours were not wasted after all (. . . laying in gold ore to be mined later).

But I haven't got any real pleasure out of writing: it's like belching or expelling gas: it's something you do to feel better after.

AN EVER-INCREASING indulgence of all things human.

HOME IS A CRACKED GLASS, shattered by time, and to look back toward it is to see the pieces of yourself clear and distinct.

MY FIRST AIRPLANE TRIP — from San Antonio to Dover, Delaware, in a military cargo plane — is an exercise in seeing-and-assimilation. I look down at St. Louis and say to myself: Well, that's St. Louis, and I try to soak up the deep St. Louis-ness of the scene. I stare hard at the Mississippi River nearby, trying to grasp that idea too — *the Mississippi, over there, right now.* When I lose sight of it, I try next to be equal to Ohio, where we land and spend the night.

. . . Ohio — and all those Middle American trees beyond the

runway as our plane takes off the following morning. I look out the window and think about "America" and how "Ohio" is part of "America": I think about people already at work in the small buildings off to the side of the runway among the many receding trees — people who are "Ohioans" — and I try to feel how it is to be a person going about his routines at ten minutes after eight, Ohio-time, on a morning in May. . . . Clouds fill my window constantly and the cargo plane keeps bumping and swaying over who-knows what cities and states and mountain ranges and then, finally, we land in Dover. I listen to strange accents in the downtown bus terminal, and soon I am on a night-time bus ride past factories with many windows. They are history-book factories to me, for I am in that heartland of the East that everyone has read about as a child, the place where history-book America was. I do not consider the grimness that those windows suggest; my thoughts are the ordinary ones any visitor would have on his first trip there as he bounces on his bus seat in darkness. I see the factories — and know that Washington and Pennsylvania and Maryland are no longer just names in books and on maps but are actual presences nearby. People who are Pennsylvanians — who buy Pennsylvania-baked bread and trade in Pennsylvania drug stores — are asleep this very moment in Pennsylvania homes. . . .

And then, at ten o'clock, I am in New York itself: a city whose streets have been walked on by the famous few and the unknown many. It is one of the fabled cities of the world and I, improbably, am there — smelling New York air and seeing New York stores and wondering how much I will be changed in the morning when I look in a New York mirror.

SURELY THERE ARE TRUTHS. Surely truth is not simply the sum total of all *beliefs*. Take religion: you cannot really be tolerant in religious matters if you believe in truth. A person cannot be a believing Baptist and a believing Catholic and a believing Buddhist at the same time. Yet how can he unswervingly keep one belief knotted in his fist when he knows that millions of others are believing — just as devoutly as he — in something else? Somebody is *wrong* as far as *truth* goes, even though he may be quite right as far as his *belief* goes. Thus millions are all wet as far as the truth goes yet worship in perfect bliss. They *believe* in what they are doing.

How do you ever adopt a belief for yourself in the middle of a mess like this? How do you ever find a faith that survives the basic contradictions between the formal world religions? How do you keep from being, all the days of your life, just another hound of heaven sniffing an eternally cold trail?

I LISTENED TO MYSELF pro-ing and con-ing, weighing and rejecting. I was like a naturalist observing tropical fighting fish swim around and around in a small clear bowl, nipping at each other's fins.

DESIRE, the key to living, the ingredient absolutely necessary to the continuance of a deep and full life. To *want* something: it keeps you in motion. It makes you lean forward. (Sadness: the absence of any real desire. It is awareness of the fact that you once *did* have desires, strong and healthy.)

IT MUST BE REMEMBERED that all my tentative forays into the profound are conditioned by these central facts: 1) I am too alone; 2) while alone, I try to establish disciplines which will enable me to function properly as a lone person and not end up doing a wild and irresponsible act.

Thus I probably overstate my case about many matters.

I AM ASTOUNDED by the number of people trying to do the right thing. It seems a shame that having good intentions isn't a virtue (—all these people, both dull and brilliant, working within the cell block of their good intentions).

I CAN NEVER evaluate my own thoughts and feelings, can

never tell how worthy they are. I just know I put them down because they are sincere. And sincerity is a deafening noise. Its huge absorbing sound deafens you to the worth and meaning of what you say and think. This is why a writer or crusader seeks out others for their reactions — not because he doubts for a minute his own convictions but because all he can hear is the noise of his own honest blast. He must find out if anyone else can hear that blast, too.

IN THE WEST PASTURE of the ranch there is a wooded ravine that begins at an old dry waterfalls and casually winds southward into lower country. It is a kind of sanctuary, and on summer days, when the earth seems bent on purging and punishing itself unmercifully in the hot open grassy places, the ravine runs within its boundaries of tall trees with almost priestly ease, like a slim quiet river of shade. Sun filters down through the heavy post oaks and lies in contented yellow patches on fallen leaves. And in hidden places down the way doves, overcoming the pleasant inertia of silence within the ravine, will volunteer again and again their crooning sounds of saddened love.

HOLE IN THE BLUFF: It was a cold November afternoon in Austin, and I watched a little girl dig at a hole in the white caliche bluff that stretched behind her apartment house. She had on white mittens, and wore red corduroy trousers and a red coat with a hood. She was very pretty.

She dug at the hole with a stick, doing it very lady-like and with precision. Her free arm was bent a little at her side, swinging in a balancing rhythm. Every so often she gently laid her stick on the ground and with her mittened hand cleaned out the hole with care. She seemed to love the hole in the bluff and she talked to it as she cleaned; she treated it as her silent friend there in the cold and dreary back yard.

She had been playing at the bluff for a long while when a back door opened in the apartment house and a woman half-stuck her head out. She asked the little girl what in the world she was doing out there. She called for the little girl to come inside, waited a moment while she withdrew her head, then with her head fully outside again she called, Now do you *hear* me, Carolyn? and slammed the door.

The little girl kept digging, as though she were going to pay no attention to her mother. Then finally she quit. She put the stick down and began scooping up the loose caliche and putting it back into the hole. When she finished she patted the hole and looked at it and leaned over so that she could lay her cheek flat against it. She held her cheek there briefly and drew back and patted the hole a final time and and started slowly across the yard toward her back door. As she walked she looked down at her white-buckle shoes as they slid along beneath her through the yellow winter grass. Then after climbing the steps of the small back porch and touching the mop, the broom, and the garbage can with her mitten, she opened the back door of her mother's apartment and went inside.

COLLEGE: For me, it was reading Turgenev in a tree on Saturday afternoon near the stadium while the football crowd sent up periodic roars. It was standing in downtown Austin on Sunday morning, looking at passing faces. But at first it was just standing at a stop light at two o'clock on a warm afternoon and not quite being able to shake off the feeling that something was out of kilter, that I ought not to be anywhere at that hour except in a classroom: I was not quite free from the previous twelve years of public schooling which had taught me that two o'clock in the afternoon *belonged* to school: it was a *school hour* (. . . that sudden college unstructuredness; that subtle freeing of hours-of-the-day and giving them back to the world outside school buildings).

NO ONE ALLOWS HIMSELF to fully praise a man who looks at life with a negative eye. It is deep in the nature of our being to give the universe a plus mark, regardless of how little it seems to deserve such a mark during the living of our daily lives, and that essential plusness must somehow be affirmed by a man to whom we would give our deepest trust.

We cannot help but follow the lead of the man who lives a mortal life, as we do, and then ends up giving it his blessing. Much as we seek them out to hear their side, we do not wish to adopt the credos of those brilliant cripples who are too much maimed in their dealings with life. A complainer is only half a man, we feel, for complaining is what we all can do. We are always on the lookout for those special ones who surmount the circumstances of their lives, who endure, who are made of some kind of special stuff that does not chip or crack in the wild heats of living.

(Oh, we will stick long times with the brilliant complainers: we will marvel as they take their scalpel-crutches and lance the running sores of heaven and earth; we will shake our heads in great bobs of agreement as they blow their acid breaths against old false gods. But we will not reach for the hand of the complainer and say: shake, brother, you have said it. We will nod in his direction, respectfully, and then turn away; for he is too charged with little minus signs. We go back to raising our eyes and searching heavenward again for something enduring and solid and real, some Great Positive — something like what religious people say they have when they speak confidently of the Cross.)

DISTANT COWS EATING on the side of a grassy knoll: black hatchet blades driven into the earth.

IF I WERE a Humorist department: develop the picture of the conscientious writer who takes pencil, paper, and flashlight to bed with him nightly to catch those penetrating but oh-so-fleeting midnight thoughts. (By the time he finds the flashlight, the thought has gone. Flashlight keeps rolling off the bed. He wakes up the middle of the night, wide-eyed: is it the long-awaited-for vision? No, it is a pencil in his back. Paper gets rolled and soggy with sweat. Sometimes he stays awake for hours; no thoughts come.

Sheepish, but diligent.)

ANXIETY, I BELIEVE, is the only channel through which love sails. The lover, always wanting to suddenly gain what cannot be readily possessed, is awakened, lured, hooked by anxiety. Where there is doubt, there is also interest. Where there is immediate certainty, there lurks the danger of boredom (I write truisms like suddenly discovered truths). For if one thing is certain about love, it is that one wishes first to love, not be loved; it is only after having an object to lavish one's love upon that the lover demands to be loved in return. Thus, it is the order of events, not the events themselves, that count.

The wisdom of the ages seems to be that there is always one who is the lover and one who is loved. I haven't liked this idea. I have wanted to improve on human nature, or deny it.

MY SCENES AND SKETCHES: lyric attempts only, suspended almost always in the pale aqueous solution of late afternoon sunlight; caresses on paper by a crooning pen; evocations of a vigorless cameo-ed world.

I WANTED TO *love* GOD, as I had loved or tried to love everything else. But I couldn't work it that way. It seemed that to be in the proper swing of things you had to back up, cool off, straighten your tie, brush the sweaty hair out of your feverish eyes, and *be nice* to God, be respectful and courteous, since the relationship betweeen creator and subject is to be considered a decorous and rather impersonal one, what with his being *God* and all. The less you were preoccupied with God — the less you were *truly concerned* — why, the more pure of heart you were and the better your mental health. "You're trying to *understand* God!" one lady said, with insight, meaning: YOU BETTER STOP THAT RIGHT QUICK: YOU BETTER GO BACK TO HOEING IN YOUR OWN GARDEN AND CONFINE YOURSELF TO MAKING PLEASANT COM-

MENTS NOW AND THEN ABOUT HOW THE LILIES DON'T TOIL
OR HAVE CONCERN FOR THEIR RAIMENT (AND ABOVE ALL
THEY DON'T ASK QUESTIONS: THAT'S THEIR MAIN FORTE).

To try to *know* was the sin, the blockage, the alienation. It was
all primarily a matter of human impertinence, an absence of the
prostrating spirit, a matter of "pride." To be nicely and comfortably normal, one should want to take his God like bedtime Oval-
tine: lukewarm.

I WAS JUST SITTING THERE in a chair when I started scar-
ing myself at the phenomenon of *thought*. Soon I was trying to
listen to myself think, wondering how that wild bunch of chemi-
cals and neurons upstairs ever made any sense.

(Do they move down the dark convolutions of the brain carefree and eager, like a flock of French boarding school girls laughing and giggling their way down long hallways; or do they move
silently, sure-footed and skilled, like rats racing at night along the
familiar ropes of some isolated ship?)

THE READING BOOK for my eighth grade class has a story
in it with these words: ". . . from broken-hearted misery to bursting happiness."

I looked at them yesterday as if I were looking at snapshots of
old, forgotten friends. These were words I once could have used
to describe the range of my own feelings, for I once lived, too, in
a climate of extremes.

But how strange and distant the words appear now. It is as if
some time ago I stepped out of the road of passions and came to
rest in a pasture of temperance. No deep urges, no wild moments,
no fierce desires. My emotional pendulum has ceased the giddy
swing from ecstasy to despair. It now arcs with uneventful re-
gularity from mild despair to mild despair, with the sound of an
old horse clopping on a deserted street.

WHY DOES A PERSON WRITE? This question, more and

more, becomes the important one for me. When someone tells me he writes, I want to stare at him hard and ask: what do you know, what have you found out? And if you have found something out, why must you run put it down on paper? Why don't you just keep it in your head and *know* it? And do you plan to keep writing down all the things you know, all your life?

IF IN THE SUDDEN smell of rain there is not manifestation of divinity on earth, well, there's no use trying to envision heaven.

RANCH PEOPLE: I cannot help liking the idea of them, their lives.

Just the other day I cut out a photograph from the *Sheep and Goat Raisers* magazine. A young rancher near San Saba had won a prize for taking care of his range properly — something like that — and the family was shown posing in their ranch front yard: the neat young wife, a couple of yellow-haired kids, the thick-bodied, slightly balding young rancher in his sport shirt and khakis. The yard gate was ajar between the two rock posts, a collie was lying on the grass, flowers bordered the front of the house, oak trees were in the background.

There he was, in the country, in front of his home, with his family: a man who had become a prize winner because he took care of his range. . . .

THE DAYS PASS, and I take no beauty from them.

WHAT IS HARDEST to remember — and what, above all else, must be remembered — is to be skeptical when reading the skeptical.

TWO WOMEN in high heels and dark glasses sit at a little table in a riverside cafe in San Antonio. They are both reading. Now and then one of them taps her long cigarette absentmindedly in the ash tray but keeps on reading as she returns the cigarette carefully to her mouth. The Mexican waitresses, carrying steaming trays of food, weave past their table for an hour or more, but the women never look up. And a big Mexican man with excellent teeth and a broad black sombrero lets songs leap passionately from his throat and tharum-tharums on his guitar and jingles the bells on his pearl-gray mariachi pants—but the women apparently do not hear him. At least they do not pay him any mind. Instead, they cross and recross their legs thoughtfully (and you can almost feel the sensuous scrape of expensive nylons one against the other) and tap their cigarettes and drink their beer and read their books entitled GOD IS LOVE.

MY THOUGHTS, no matter how often or how much I castigate them, shame them, spur them, never fall into the pattern and consistency I want them to have. I want them to analyze the events and people I have seen and crystallize them into stories. I want them to make a Harvard outline, and assign meanings, directions, values. But no: they caper; they weasel. They mock my big demands.

Thus I have never been able to make anything on a suitably big scale. I have simply trapped the transient little thoughts which dart through me and out again. Little aphorisms, little sketches, little pronouncements — I pretend they are sudden shafts down to worthy ore. But I know they are like sundry bits of -ites and -oxides in a schoolboy's rock collection: the ones he can never mold together into a solid gold coin that will ring when thumped or will resist a good hard bite. They remain there in his desk, charming perhaps in their own way, always ready for inspection — but too varied, not of a piece. (What one needs is all zinc or all silver or all gold. And you cannot get such pure and scarce materials through idle collecting here and there. You have to set up camp and get out all your costly machinery and mine, mine, mine.)

MOMENTS OF CRASHING INSIGHT reveal nothing, really,

except how useless such moments are in themselves. For they merely throw into dramatic relief the rest of one's life — showing how impossible it would be to live out all the countless hours except at a purely animal, reflex level. (A life composed only of insights: like a hen continually laying beautiful, multi-colored glass eggs.)

ON KATHERINE ANNE PORTER: There seems to be a curious lack of breath and air in much of her work — a dry feeling, as if her words were too lacking in juices. There is no osmotic flow between the words and the experiences from which they were born. It is as though the stories were solely a product of her brain instead of that indefinable mixture of body and brain and spirit that apparently is the source of most good writers' creations.

I do not have any quarrel with the continual applauding of her work: I just do not find myself compelled to read her. (And when I do read her stories I find myself involved in a subdued and gentlemanly relationship: she remains there inside her book, contained within the carefully chosen words, and I remain there in my chair — at a distance, not particularly involved.)

Is it a lack of richness, of vitality, of verve that I seem to miss? Is it that I will grant her work the perfection of a Swiss watch — but then claim the right not to care too much for Swiss watches? (I was once very glad to come across Somerset Maugham saying what I had always felt but never quite had the self-assurance to believe or express: that a thing of beauty is *not* a joy forever; that its very perfection soon bores since it has excluded from itself the minor flaws that make something interesting and full of life.)

Sometimes it seems that in her strenuous effort to reach perfection of statement she squeezes the spark of life out of a story and all we have left are the carefully measured words (not that I'm knocking words; words, yes, let's have only the right ones. But let's also have the feelings, too, jammed above and around and under and behind the words. Steinbeck and Faulkner and Hemingway do precisely this sort of backgrounding in their best stories:

you read the words, but as you do so there are unseen, unexpressed yet nevertheless palpable feelings crawling off the page onto your own sensibilities).

I will gladly walk past a Katherine Anne Porter exhibit in some museum of art — observing the small card which says, The Works of a Master Story Teller. But I will not complain to the curator that the books are beyond my touch under glass — for that's where they have always been.

I BELIEVE THAT everyone wants to surrender, wants to get rid of his self and worship the one or One who would take that self off his hands. The self weighs; it is a genuine cross.

SOMETIMES I LOOK at an oak tree at noon, off at a distance and making a shade, and I cannot honestly consider it to be less alive than a human.

SITTING IN ALL its purity on the nice display cloth of the mind, experience many times shows but a single facet. Cut and put into place by Memory, that canny jeweler, it shines for us with its bright diamond glow: The Good Thing, Lost Forever.

SOME PEOPLE accept God all their lives. It seems I am to spend all my life hunting for Him.

THERE COME these moments when you have to doff your mortal hat and say: Everything is perfect. And you have to say these words out loud to properly express your awe.

You see, you have been stumbling around examining this thought and that, throwing them all away and trying still another one; then you find one you think is worthy keeping. Like an elated Truth prospector, you drop your pick and shovel and grab this fine new thought from the ground and examine it, rub it clean, then look closely at it from all angles. Yes, indeed: it is a good one, you decide. Then you begin to look not just at it but *into* it, and that's when this hat doffing routine begins — when you stand open-mouthed and say your words out loud. For you suddenly see that this thing, this nugget, is not something *you* are responsible for, that *you* should preen your feathers about. It is simply one of the timeless perfect things of this world have you have *perceived.* You have found yourself staring headlong at part of the Big Plan again. That's what scares you, realizing that this thing you stumbled on *had* to be there all along. The Plan could not have been the Plan without it. The world could not have waited for you to come along and discover something and then begin the demonstrate the truth of it.

Holding your discovered Something in your hand, you realize that nothing has been left out: the scope and depth of the Plan is achingly profound. So immediately you say, All right, with such a Plan there *is* meaning; and you turn, wanting to see, finally, the rest of it, the Whole. But there is nothing to see. And you look quickly down at your bright new thought — that glowing manifestation of the Big Revelation you sought — and you see that the fire inside has burned down, the luster has faded, and it is like any common ore of the earth. There is no truth left in it anymore.

(The "discovery" of such a "truth" is like an explorer grimly hacking through jungle undergrowth to find a New Way West, and suddenly crashing out upon a super highway and a shopping center.)

THE JAUNDICED FELLOW: He finally had the drop on them now because he wasn't having any more, thank you. No, sir, no more passionate dealings with life; no more fancy involvements. He had his downturned mouth and his afternoon chair on the porch and his grim abiding outlook. That was enough. And as for those others out there — those big doers and going-Jessies, those wide-eyed innocent greyhounds still panting around after their mechanical rabbits — well, all he could say was have at it and welcome to it. He wasn't about to distribute Wise-Up pills. If they wanted to keep sweating and jabbing at thin air — wanted to keep right on thinking that with just a little more time and a little more luck they could cut out for themselves a nice-sized piece of glory — let 'em. He was beyond that now. He couldn't be bothered.

CHRISTMAS in the hill country: dark, wet trunks of oak trees rising above sensationally green winter grass.

EVERY TIME I HEAR or see or read something worthy, the old mortar and pestle inside starts grinding: *I* want to do something worthy, too.

AN INTERESTING POINT: "Do you want to *do* or simply *have done?* . . . want to write or *have written?*"

WE — I — KEEP ASKING: is there a purpose for Man, for Me? Well, is there a purpose for spiders? I see none beyond the simple purpose of their continuing to act like spiders. Their purpose is to *be spiders.*

Are we different, any more than cats are different, from spiders, as far as a purpose goes? Spiders and cats go on being what they are, for whatever it is worth to them. But we humans, with reflective intelligences: we are not content with *being.* We question where we are going and why we came. Cats don't. They do what cats have always done, and so do spiders. They roam through weeds or hang from threads, and are content.

What could possibly be man's purpose? He assumes — through viewing his heritage and noticing his present supremacy on earth — that he has some special place, some special end and significance: some *purpose* that, though inscrutable to him, is one not assigned to cats and spiders. Yet if we suppose that a cat's "purpose" is simply to be fully that unique creature he is — a fur licker and a graceful mover — then we might suppose that a man's purpose is likewise to be himself in all *his* uniqueness: to be the one special being that can wonder, imagine, strive, hope, and search —

especially into the farthest limits of all things of which he can conceive.

However, there is something wrong here. A cat's purpose brings him contentment. He seldom wants to do things other than cat-things; he thus carries the mantle of catliness rather lightly. Similarly, the spider seems to go right along with its destiny: it does not sit on a log and mope, refusing to spin. It does not rage against having a tail end full of silk. The burden of being a spider is not more than what a spider can rightly bear. But a human: he seems to find a certain *weight* in being that which he is, and would many times alter the structure of life because it does not make for one vital condition: his happiness.

The cat, now, is neither happy nor unhappy; he simply *is* and thrives on being that way. He cannot conceive of a different life for himself. Yet if a human is the only living creature that can evaluate his own state and perhaps find it wanting, does this intellectual capacity alone imply the presence of some special *purpose,* some essential *godliness?* Is a man more like God than a cat is simply because he alone can feel unhappy and unfulfilled and therefore strives out of this discomfort to be more like something else (that "something else" being God)?

Setting aside the possibility of "becoming more like God," can we say that there is more *of* God in a man than in a spider? Is man more *like* God than a spider is? Some have said — mainly those expansive old pantheists — that God *is in all things;* He *is* all things. Well, now, if God is not some special unit, some separate force, but instead the total of *all* things — spiders, cats, men — what is a man striving after with his "special purpose"? He cannot be *more Godly* since he, along with the rest of living things, is already part of God.

Is he, perhaps, to strive to be more fully himself, more *man-ly?* Is this his responsibility, just as a cat's "responsibility" might be to act more *cat-ly* (— ignoring the fact that man's striving involves a sense of constant unfulfillment, as opposed to the cat's sense of constant contentment). Or will we simply have to say, after all, that there was no special creation of man, and therefore no special function? Will we be obliged to recognize that the range of all living things is like the range of the spectrum: just as there are bright colors and somber colors and many intermediate shades, so are there many living forms on a huge evolutionary scale, ranging from primitive to advanced, each with a special nature but none with a special calling, none more Godly or divine or favored in the universe than any other?

I AM A BARNACLE, deep at sea. To live, I must join myself to something — lay myself carefully against it, meeting its every edge.

I LISTEN TO THE impressive silence within my rooming house. Nothing disturbs the sense of Sunday silence.

Through the window I can see two cats sleeping beside a coiled garden hose.

I listen and remember how as a child it was just this kind of quietness which first made me aware that I was alive — which caused me to realize that something powerful and elusive was going on in the world that I didn't understand.

As I watch, a long patch of fading sun stretches through the gathering shadows of the yard — the last corridor of afternoon light. I look at it, and it is like seeing straight into childhood: into a deep and subtle assertion of quiet earth.

IN BETWEEN HALVES at the basketball game Joe Graham leans over on the cold drink counter. At fifteen he is not waiting for anything or doing anything; he has just finished his coke and just *is*. I watch him, intrigued.

. . . He is ready and available for any sensation. He idles for a moment with an empty paper cup — not absently, as a person does when he is trying to kill time, but attentively, as though perfectly content during his moment of inspection. Then he leans forward a bit beyond the counter and looks at something — maybe a curiously shaped bit of popcorn, a dropped hairpin, a faded bronze hinge on a cabinet. He becomes a study in potential energy, for he looks out of a genuine curiosity — with an almost muscular tautness. The life force that pulses in him demands that he respond directly, immediately, at all times, to his surroundings — to the perception of whatever is suddenly new and compelling.

Joe Graham, a schoolboy figure seen from behind, a vital parcel of 15-year-old energy, full-charged, dynamic.

Joe Graham: life on display at the cold drink counter.

I WILL NEVER WRITE a story, I guess. I remember, am concerned with, totally unimportant details: how the sun looked in the late afternoon against the face of Gregory gym (— vaguely flushed, as if the wall had begun to run a mild collegiate fever); how a tow sack looked wrapped around a water hydrant in December; how a bug crawled on a hackberry trunk on Saturday afternoon.

Stories, of course, seldom stop for bugs, or knot-holes in boards, or chicken droppings — trivial things. Stories are always going some place. They have an artistic purpose to fulfill. . . . But me — I have not been able to figure out any of life's proper values and therefore I have not developed clear, artistic purposes. I had just as soon stop for a bug, or chicken droppings, as for a Raskolnikov because life has not yet proved to me that it values any one creation more than it does another.

MEMORIES ARE like spoiled children and if you don't have a reason to discipline them — that is, if you don't have a plan for them — they will run around loose in your head, knocking against one another, all of them demanding to be let out and play.

IS WRITING REALLY a form of art? Why not call it a form of psychiatry, or philosophy, or sociology, or religion? What, exactly, is a person trying to do when he writes?

THERE GRADUALLY CAME upon me in early adolescence a monstrous feeling of *being alive and not knowing what to do about it*. It was a feeling of impotence, I suppose, an inability to do a valuable, meaningful act when faced with the hugeness of the world.

IT'S GOT TO BE my way in writing — with my eyes and my body — or it will never be any good. Now, if only I had a "way" that I could believe in, I would work at it joyfully.

THE STORY OF ANY MAN, any person, is a strange and delicate thing.

SHE'S A GIRL, fifteen, and the possessor of bigger-than-average breasts. So what does she do? Why, she puts on tight pink pants, dyes her brown hair blond, and within the year pursues her sad little way into marriage with a fellow who has two tattoos and keeps his pack of cigarettes inside the rolled-up sleeve of his white T-shirt.

I DON'T THINK I am *interested* in God as such; it's just that, having a mind, I feel logically compelled to find Him. It's like being involved in reading a fine book: a tremendous desire arises in you to know who wrote it and to stare into his face; but all the while, despite the looking, it is the thing that he did you are attracted to. The creator can never match his creation, if the creation is any good.

LONELINESS BRINGS one's passions and preoccupations to the surface. If the person can deal with them fairly, as well as with the words at his command, sometimes he ends up with literature on his hands.

MOST COLLEGE EDUCATION COURSES are so simple-minded they are like obstacle courses designed for paraplegics.

IT WAS SUNDAY AFTERNOON, and I lay on my bed, having

rejected all possible solutions for salvaging the rest of the day. I had said no to self-improvement, no to self-indulgence, no to self-obliteration. I was simply there on the bed at two o'clock with an inert body and a mind out of gear: with my *self*, a familiar commodity to which I assigned no value.

It was like buying the last ticket to the last empty desert island: there on the beach I lay, surrounded by miles of vacant green water; without a raft or tool or piece of bread to eat: just me, on an infinitely still place.

WILL I JUST go through life chronicling my weaknesses and laments?

I CAN NEVER find the peace to forget writing, yet I can't find the compelling vision which would enable me to really begin. I hop about like Mr. Hulot, peering, gaping, poking into life, never with any real consistency or purpose.

MY SOUL DOES not remain anguished long enough. The torments that play over me ultimately find release through the safety valves of my too-damned-healthy system. I am not goaded into great bursts of creative fury. I am such a temperate bastard.

HOT SUMMER DAYS, when you lie sunning on a raft at Landa Park; when you eat a ham sandwich on toast at a Walgreen drugstore and watch the blades of a ceiling fan move slowly around; when your eyes are sandy and sleepy and the world is covering its mouth in a long summer yawn.

THAT REMEMBERED FEELING from childhood: that there was a God in the world, watching, quietly taking note; that there was Someone who knew all and approved and disapproved.

Such a feeling is still vaguely and deeply present with me today. I still find myself silently engaged in a dialogue with the air which, though ostensibly empty, contains that old *something* outside myself which I cannot ignore. I still, by reflex, make a quick, minimal acknowledgement of this presence during the day — thus never being truly free, always having to mentally trot over like a sub checking in with the referee and then proceeding on down the field.

I SEEMED TO WANT an altar to lay my body on.

SMALL OLD NEGRO PORTERS: Wearing clean khakis and wide gray suspenders, they move about on early Saturday mornings in the corridors of cool, darkened municipal buildings in San Antonio. They are always in laborious transit, carefully nursing along a mop or broom or dust pan from its temporary quarters beside an elevator to its permanent home in the utility room down the hall — moving with both arms bent, one hand grasping the broom or dust pan and the other flapping backwards with each step as if mildly swimming: old Negro men who somehow manage to convey the notion that if they haven't just finished with a cigarette they are going to be at one right away, just as soon as they can make it down the hall. Or actually better than that: who manage to keep smoking all the time — all day long, every day — who right now have hidden in their cupped hand, like a talisman, a fragment of a cigarette they have babied down the elevator and through the morning pleasantries of the buoyant allergy specialist — the cigarette that will not only make it down the hall but, the Lord willing, can make it clear through until nine o'clock when the candy girl in the lobby opens her counter and lets a man have — on the cuff — a brand new pack of Luckies.

THINGS THAT are good to feel with your hands: a stick of fireplace wood, freshly sawed; a fish just out of water, size one pound; the cold head of a hammer; a football.

I MUST FIND a home of my own. I have been a visitor too long. I have observed, taken stock, reflected; but I can do it no

more. I can ride in my car no more, and walk in the late afternoon
— alone — no more. I must make a break and take root somewhere. I must dedicate myself; I must *begin.*

But I need a reason to work, a reason to exist from day to day.
I need a plan, a goal. I need things to grow tired over at the end
of the day.

I want a song to sing.

I want a trail leading somewhere. I want the ambition and purpose and dedication in my life that makes doctors doctors and
actors actors and communists communists. I want to work. I want
to sweat and be concerned. I want to get on a bandwagon and
believe in something strongly. I want to be a partisan.

I don't want to be an onlooker any more. I am tired of walking
around in other people's homes, toying with objects in their front
rooms, looking out their windows — restless in being a visitor but
having no place to go. I am tired of hunting for meaning and purpose and peace. I am tired of being anguished, of being jailed
within myself.

I want to taste the freedom that comes from getting down to
work.

CYPRESS CREEK ROAD: I drive along, seeing the country
stretch out into the morning, and I become limp with the sense of
greenery and peace and sun and air. The simple magnificence of
trees, of bird-sounds, of grasses — it washes over me, possesses me,
makes me joyful and clean.

I look at the narrow road left over, undisturbed, from the '30s,
with grass growing into it from the roadside; at the Spanish oaks
and pecan trees taking all the shining ten o'clock light into their
leaves; at weeds along the creek and prickly poppies in the field,
at cattails and gourd vines and clumps of hoarhound and cedar
posts and windmills and a farmhouse partly hidden in a distant
joining of hills. These things I see clearly, and yet I do not understand what feelings I can express about them. It is as though I
want to say, without knowing why, that . . . *nature never lacks,* it

never fails to satisfy, it is the only paradise which I am always ready to enter.

THOSE WERE the quivering, questing days when I assumed there were solutions loose in the world, and when I was out to find them.

NEVER BEING without that sense of . . . what — of children dancing on graves; a sense of never-ending innocence and mystery.

ALTHOUGH it does matter somewhat about Don Quixote and Hamlet and Faust, it matters very much more about *you*.

IN THOSE DAYS I wanted God. Perhaps I wanted the very air to suddenly speak to me, or my thoughts to go humming out of my head to meet a holy velvet.

I didn't know exactly *what* to want, except some kind of manifestation out of the maddening silence. *God*: the very sound of the word was emotional. Three letters summing up all.

In those great wanting' days was it just immaturity — like a schoolboy's crush on a heavenly Jack Armstrong? Was I running around, spoiled, wanting not God but some kind of divine crutch?

What is God-seeking? Why do some seek and some not? If I had had no deep personal problems to concern myself with, would I have tried to relate myself to a God?

SELF-CRITIQUE, Vol. XXXXIV, Chapter 14, Book 7: It is time you realized where your writing talents begin and end. You are no short story writer; that much is plain. You have neither the desire nor knack to create characters.

You are, if anything, a worry-wart with a pencil. An impressionist. Perhaps there actually does breathe in you some poetic instinct, which you satisfy with your brief bursts. Perhaps you can present a mood or moment clearly. But you have as yet demonstrated no real skill as a prose artist. You certainly show no ability to sustain any work beyond a page or two. And as a thinker — well, I don't get the idea that you're any particular heavyweight.

What *is* on your side? Perhaps it is simply this: a desire to think about life, a concern for the varied events that a person is involved with during his lifetime, plus a recognition that it is fruitless to blow-up a thought into something more than it really is (thus your tendency to write only a few lines about a scene or thought: you know it would be a form of dishonesty to go beyond the limit of your brief telling and try to support a more impressive structure with hollow stilts of dramatic stuff that you don't really feel).

There is no real maturity in you yet. So don't strain to inject false "knowledgeability" into writing simply to take advantage of whatever talent you may have. If you have a small talent, stay true to it; don't ruin it by attempting to go beyond it.

OUTSIDE IRENE'S: At eight in the morning the town itself — a casual collection of small stores and vacant lots full of July weeds — seems barely awake, barely willing to straddle the highway for another hot and uneventful South Texas day. But out at the junction a dozen cars and trucks are nosed in toward Irene's Cafe. Some of the cars are big and roughly used, undercoated with red mud from oil field leases; others, like the bright red Chevrolet of the linen supply man, are slim and polished. The Shell distributor's car is there, and the deputy sheriff's with its high, whip-like aerial.

As the dusty screen door opens and bangs shut three route salesmen come outside: the Schlitz man, the Sunbeam bread man, the Morton's Potato Chip man. The door bangs again and they are joined by a vending machine man in a limp white shirt. They stand for a while, snapping cigarette lighters closed, clearing their throats, squinting vaguely at the sky. Then they start for their cars.

"Catch you next time for the coffee, Rich."

"Sure thing . . . Roy, Bill, now yawl be good."

"Try to."

They jerk brief nodding farewells, back their cars across the gravel, and head down the road to Three Rivers — all except the vending machine man who continues to linger in front of the doorway, smoking his cigarette and frowning. He is a thin-waisted man with a worn belt and a careful roach to his hair. Standing there in the early morning sunlight he seems to be listening to something in his thoughts, something that mildly disturbs him — something, possibly, that a vending machine man should not even be aware of on such an ordinary, work-day morning. As he stares into his vision he puffs his cigarette deeply, slowly drawing in his cheeks.

But just then the Barnett's Fried Pie salesman comes out of Irene's, blowing his nose, and the vending machine man quickly covers his moment of privacy. He turns and flashes a wide, welcoming smile with his horselike teeth.

"Well," he says, "gonna be another scorcher." The pie salesman nods, fans his fleshly nose mechanically with his handkerchief — as if his handkerchief were a featherduster and he was carefully cleaning merchandise — and walks on around the side of the cafe.

The vending machine man drops his cigarette into the gravel and rubs at it with his shoe — gently, almost fondly, as if it were the germ of a life that did not quite get born. He clears his throat, starts to spit, thinks better of it, and moves on toward the door of his company car. He gets in quickly and drives away.

THERE IS A SPECIAL TREE in my memory — one that never sheds a leaf and apparently will never die. It has some kind of meaning for me, but I do not know what.

It is a chinaberry tree of my childhood, in a yard several blocks away from home. I went there one time with W. to visit his two friends, the Leinweber boys. I don't remember the climbing or any other details; I don't even know how small I was. I just remember the *sense* of us up there, in the branches. And yet, despite being sunk in such enigmatic dimness, that tree has remained one of the most compelling puzzles of my life.

Why has that one lone tree remained so huge among all the others I have known? Is it, like all mysteries, merely a combination of some kind of human ignorance and some kind of unhuman beauty or terror? If life itself were finally plumbed, would it turn out to be no more profound than a chinaberry tree — easily and correctly perceived if only we were God?

SLIM-WAISTED ANTS making their way over a landscape of finely granulated dirt. . . .

THE TYPICAL ARTIST flicks his ego out like a snake's tongue to touch his surroundings. If things feel safe he will remain a while and rattle his tail winsomely. However, if the air seems hostile he will attack blindly, without provocation, whoever is near, or else slither back haughtily into the underbrush.

WRITING IS LIKE sexual tumescence: a gradual spreading urgency finally hardening itself into a blunt demand for penetration and release. In both cases the mind is by-passed; for the moment there is simply an uncompromising desire to get out of you that which is causing such a steady pressure. Yet the mind can always cut into this pressure so suddenly that both creative and sexual force dramatically disappear, and no amount of flagellation can restore the previous edge (writing, sex: neither, then, is subject to an exercise of will. Will cannot effectively summon or control them; they are powers within themselves. They remain as strange guests — always welcome, always exciting, but quite imperious, rather godly. You take what they have to offer whenever they offer it, or not at all).

GILCREASE, on Galveston Bay: I placed the wooden chair in the shade of the cabin and then after a moment laid aside the magazine I had brought along to read. I tilted the chair back against the cabin and looked out to where the many small fiddler crabs were moving slowly across the wet sand, and I knew that there was nothing I ought to be doing that was more important than just being in that chair, looking out, while another summer day was beginning on the coast.

So I sat there, not opening the magazine, not feeling any need to escape myself through others' words or to be doing any other thing. I was satisfied to be a guest of the morning.

At the corner of the cabin black dragonflies were pulsing backwards from the grass—mosquito hawks, the tourist court manager had called them. They kept up their rhythmic feint-and-retreat against the grass while bees flew in and out of a low plum tree.

I looked past the cabin. . . . Breeze and yucca, yes, and crushed shell roads and oleander. Gulls. Piers. And the bright sunlight over all.

In front of the cabin next to mine a tanned slim girl — blond-haired, barefooted, long-legged — watched her grandmother from a green lounge chair. The woman, in slacks, was watering hollyhocks. She paused, studied the hollyhocks, tilted her watering can again while the sun streamed down and the girl sat unmoving behind sun shades and the fiddler crabs inched along the sand.

Out in the bay the water had met the morning light and held it; the bay and sky were one. A tug saluted another tug with a long low horn.

A face stared up from the cover of my magazine; a mosquito hawk came close and investigated.

I sat, breathing regularly.

I HAVE BEEN UNABLE to accept calmly that human life comes from a mere chance meeting of a wriggle-headed sperm and an inviting egg. We are asked to believe that as soon as such an idle union burgeons and erupts into self-awareness, it suddenly has eternal significance beyond the significance of the separate originating parts. Non-conscious life, chancing to combine with other non-conscious life, forms conscious life, and this supposedly translates itself into something supra-life, something eternal.

If the sperm of my father had not united with the egg of my

mother, I would not be now nor would ever have been. I would have missed life. Yet, through chance, I have been fashioned from nothing into life and am asked to assume that I am on an awesome escalator, ascending toward some infinite stability in form or spirit (— do you mean to say, then, that the difference between nothingness and eternity is the slipshod, maybe-this-time meeting of sperm and egg? One sexual intercourse less and I would not have been. . . .)

What kind of certitude can you find out of such a helter-skelter business as this? We lament those we know who died, but never lament the ones who are never born. Did God ordain the particular intercourse that fashioned me? Does God ordain whether or not a contraceptive works?

Life and death, God and chance: they're all too mixed up.

M.:

Once M. was over the mountain, in a place,
and I, at the foot of the mountain, at night
would look to the mountain as if it were
M. and say, as if she could hear, "I wonder. . . .
I wish . . .," and go on thinking in my dead space,
my mouth a downturned rind.
And later, when it was no longer just the
mountain between us but strings of consequences
and too much time, I would go on saying
"I wonder. . . . I wish. . . .," meaning the same as before.

And once too, late at night, in a dim-lit
room as M. sat asleep in a chair,
I pondered her and what she meant to me. I
looked at her a while, at the tilted resting
head shadowed in the lack of light, at the
body reposed and waiting for the time of
becoming someone's wife, and then finally
at the feet bared in sandals. I looked

and considered all that I knew and felt, and
I began to wonder how it was to kiss her feet,
quite gently, not waking her. I wanted to
and should have, but there were others in the room
and I debated too long and then she was awake
and it could not be done.
. . . I wanted to and should have, yes: acted from
the curious depth of feeling I had not known in myself
before. To have done that would mean all grace and
all light to me now — here, alone, poised in my level-voiced
emptiness.

I CAN FEEL LIFE; it is palpable. What to others is a general condition they describe — perhaps vaguely — with words is to me something corporeal, something that has a pulse. It is as though I am tied to life by an invisible umbilical cord.

DOGS: They have faded from the landscape. It used to be that as you walked down the street of a town a dog was as much in evidence as a house or tree or rock. He would be trotting diagonally across a vacant lot or nosing along behind a shed or maybe barking somewhere in the next block. But he would definitely be there — perhaps just scratching, or sleeping, or looking on, but nevertheless taking part in all the little scenes of daily life.

But who sees dogs any more. They're still around, of course, but not as free agents. They are no longer loose in the cities and roaming the land; they are no longer a creature outside human control. Gradually they have been brought to complete domestication: people now *have* them; dogs no longer exist in and for themselves. They are now tagged, inoculated, licensed, deodorized, and perhaps IBM-ed. They are like another member of the owner's family. They have their own plastic feeding bowls, their doghouse out back, their special place in the family car on an outing. They may even have a burial plot.

Dogs are healthy, sanitary, and safely leashed: another part of the natural world brought under human domination in the name of progress.

CORPUS CHRISTI late at night, with the drive-ins closing along Ocean Drive. It is sticky-hot, with no Gulf breeze. The palm trees do not move and out in the bay the water is black. Behind the drive-ins busboys in dirty white aprons and dirty hats empty trash into garbage cans. Re-opening the back doors they crunch beetles into the sidewalk with their scuffed dirty shoes.

THE PLEASANT SMELL of her skin — faintly like leaves and rough wood.

THE NOVELTY and lure of South Texas is gone. I can take the flat land no more. I have lived here for a while but with no joy. I yearn once more for my old deep love. I need the hill country. I need its woods to walk through and its varied trees. I need its creeks and its oak leaves scattered under afternoon limbs. I need its breeze to catch the thin browning weeds on a roadside and shiver them slightly on a cold day. I need its deep smell of cedar at night in November. I need the variety of land rising and falling. I need the sun white and comforting on the post oaks as they stand like sleeping live things in the pastures. I need the small magnificence of a shadow, oblong on a hillside — and tranquil — during a long summer afternoon.

POETRY IS what you see when you take one step to the side of a familiar path and look at ordinary things with suddenly extraordinary eyes.

I WAIT for this August day to present itself to me: for the trees and houses to break their afternoon silence. You see, a town, a neighborhood, a street has a quiet life of its own that goes unnoticed — separate from the lives of people. But everyone is too busy to notice. Mothers, delivery men, carpenters, boys walking to town — they do not see the life of the day because it is too familiar. It is right there before them and is therefore invisible. . . . Cars turn corners, cats cross yards, rocks sit whitely in a two o'clock glare, but they are expected, they are routine. They are ordinary sights of a day and thus no one ever sees them.

The context: that is what I am talking about. The total mood of a day or place, not just what happens to *people*. . . . The context is always taken for granted unless something happens within it — a car wreck, a sudden rainstorm. Then the day is changed by News. A man gets up from his chair on a porch, or stops his truck, or goes to the yard fence to watch, or gets on the telephone to call. People become momentarily concerned; they are aware of the day because it is no longer the day they had taken for granted.

Without obvious little dramas to distract them, people do not look at two o'clock very deeply — at the *way* an afternoon is, the *way* a street is. They travel many miles to Carlsbad Caverns, or to Yellowstone Park, but they will not look out from their own living room windows to see *this* moment of *this* day: the way the sounds of a neighborhood are when the summer wind is moving about and there are whirring insects and birds and drifting afternoon voices and sun glintings on carpet grass. Or just the simple sitting of buildings and plants on this earth, where we are; the deep wonder of any single moment.

. . . One window in the side of any house is a mystery — one tree trunk, one door slamming, one glimpse of sky.

QUESTIONS ON FREEDOMS and responsibilities:

What concerns should be — and are — truly mine? How involved must I be with others' problems (and how detached from them is it my privilege to be)?

Should I be true to my talents and interests — to myself — even if they run counter to what I consider my responsibilities to be?

Are feelings of guilt simply to be accepted, as thorns in the side of an otherwise healthy organism (thorns that are not truly a part of the organism) — or should they be regarded as the nagging voices of a higher conscience (thorns that, simply by being lodged in the flesh, cannot be ignored — are pa.t of any life of the organism because they are undeniably there).

Do I feel guilty that I am not leading a life of greater social involvement? To what extent is every human obligated to work for what he considers to be the social betterment of mankind?

Of what am I a keeper — my brother, or myself and my own specific, private desires and talents? (And who *is* my brother? Who isn't?)

Say that there is a poor and hungry man across town (but there have always been, and always will be, poor and hungry men . . .). Should I feed him if I know about him, or should I say, with a shrugging sigh: Yes, it's all too bad, but I'm not God. I didn't set up this kind of world in which a man can go hungry — a world of plagues and diphtheria and cancer. When I feed this man, will I not see that his neighbor is hungry or sick or in need of shoes — and his neighbor's neighbor? Was I born to spend my life feeding and clothing my neighbors (and yet, can I be other than cold-blooded if I refuse to try)?

Do others solve such dilemmas by simply being unaware of them — or by being sufficiently enthralled by the world of themselves that they never seriously consider entering any other?

Could Faulkner have been serious: "The 'Ode on a Grecian Urn' is worth any number of old ladies"?

What is a work of art worth — or a single human life?

If Shakespeare saw suffering and pain and famine all around him — and did not lift a finger to alleviate it but kept on writing instead: was he justified in doing so since it turned out that he was, indeed, Shakespeare?

Had Christ possessed the talent of a Keats or Shelley, what would he have done — fed the multitudes or written sonnets about them?

JUST ONCE, I would like to write a story that would achieve the effect of Charlie Parker playing "Everything Happens to Me."

There is no mood comparable to it — that bittersweet statement of sadness and beauty and elegance and sorrow and light.

Sometimes it seems like the cry of Prometheus Bound — the god-man tied to earth but raising his voice to the heavens; and sometimes it is like that of the American Negro himself — a black man strictured by forces around him, a man contained yet still able to deny it all — defy it all; a man able to go beyond his prison and make his song; a man who knows that in the song he is able to find the freedom, possibly even the greatness, that is denied him within his bonds.

. . . TAKING MEALS AT NIGHT in small highway cafes. Sipping coffee afterwards and watching women tourists idly turn the racks of comic postcards near the cash register, toothpicks in their hands or lolling on their lips.

. . . a person with no particular place to go, no particular place he has to be. A person, like some cold and friendless animal, glad to prolong unspoken companionships within cafes. A person glad to listen to idle conversations, glad to join momentarily in other lives.

SOME WORK from the intellect down; I suppose I work from the animal up.

SUNDOWN ON THE PEDERNALES: It is summer, and you are standing in that casual stretch of time in late afternoon when the sun is going down and the river air is so strongly peaceful that you can almost hear the greenness of the weeds along the bank. You are fishing, and from time to time you look out to where your cork is riding the surface f the water, comfortably. You do not mind too much if the cork doesn't move, for it is the atmosphere of the river that counts — the long ending of the summer day, the gnats milling in the sun-washed light, the deep presence of trees.

During the early afternoon hours you wandered along the river, fishing in the sun. You stood on big whitened rocks, watching your line drift toward the shadowed ledges and the perch that waited below. You cast out from the shade of willow trees, and from the end of logs. You stood long moments, not fishing at all. And whenever you wanted to you could look up and see the red-dirt road that curved up from the river toward the Hoenig house and you could hear the sound of Mr. Hoenig on his tractor — the small German man in his small straw hat, in khakis, riding tirelessly back and forth across his sunlit field, the dust following behind like an obedient German cloud.

And now, finally, the day has come to this huge resting moment. The sun is behind the trees on the opposite bank and frogs are beginning to experiment with familiar night sounds. On the ridge behind you cows are moving out of the hay fields and into the light-and-shadow of a wide pecan grove. Tails swinging, they move with easy slowness toward the shallow crossing of the river and the barns at the top of the slope.

You look again at the cork. You smell the richness of the weeds. You watch the small circles spread as fish come to the top of the water. And as you stand there beside the long sweep of the darkening river you are without motive or malice, desire or specific need. You are content to have a fishing pole in your hand and to feel the gigantic earth-peacefulness around you. There is no other place you want to be. You are in the heart of a moment, next to trees, smiling.

OTHERS SEEM to separate the business of God from the business of life, never fusing the two. God remains as that outer-space figure who once Created and is now sitting off in some judicial place, taking note of Right and Wrong. He is for people to pray to, an Old Testament Jehovah who is more frequently displeased than pleased. Floods, earthquakes, the movement of their bowels: these are not connected with God, because He is the Eternal Distant One: He is Morality and Formality.

Life, on the other hand, is what these people *live,* a wild chaotic *present* affair not connected to some infinite plan but concerned with the workings of the earth, the atmosphere, with — in short — the Mother Nature of here and now.

It is as though the figures of the human family persist for us in the universe, raised to the last possible mathematical power: the Mother Earth concerned with the familiar daily "natural" things; the Father God, away from the routines of home but nevertheless periodically entering into one's life with some strange and righteous authority, the one who always brings about the deepest sense of solemnity and awe.

LAST NIGHT in a restaurant I watched a woman's eyes as they looked into a man's face. And as the man talked to her I watched her mouth as it began each slow trip into appreciative smiling. For the better part of thirty minutes she just sat there at the table and shone.

If someone had come up to her just then and asked, "Excuse me, please: where is your life?" she, without hesitating, without pausing a moment to think, would have turned slightly in order to face more directly the man and said, quite simply, "There."

I don't care to remember anything more about her than those eyes and the slow good warming smile and that shine in her face. It was as if everything inside her was turning very gently, like a big ferris wheel, and her heart was a small tireless engine pumping out the love necessary to keep it going.

I WANT WORDS to be of such a nature that, once they are down, there will be no more talking about them. No analyzing, no looking under the rug of my thoughts in post-mortems. I want the words to exist as things of nature, simply, directly: like clenched hands, a pair of eyes, a drop of water on a washed green leaf.

THE ONLY TRUTH, the only poetry, is that which is conceived by a single human mind as it thrusts beyond the swirl of events and sensations to say, out of a moment's reflection and isolation: This is so.

IN WRITING, I don't want to strive after a naked thought, a naked word, a naked emotion. Naked is too self-contained, existing for its own sake. It suggests the cool white marbled skin and muscle of the pure and clean Greek athlete standing in a long, soundless hallway. Naked is too much eternal form, too much above-life and beyond-life, too much frozen-beauty immobility.

I want the stuff of life in my words — neither the absolutely pure nor the flagrantly primitive. Not the perfected, emotionless and serene, nor the violently hairy and genital. My words, if there are to be any, must be scraped together from pieces of bone and air and pulsing cell — living tissues brought forth from their natural and mysterious birth. They must bring about the same feeling of reality in a person that he would get from placing his hand flat against the bark of a tree on a spring afternoon.

TRYING TO FIND my own particularly gratifying niche in the smooth continuous rock of daily living.

THE HUMAN BEING, constantly realizing his Inadequacy, constantly seeks Adequacy, which in childhood he was led to believe was God. With me this instinct, impulse is as blind and persistent as any physical passion. God, as human compulsion. . . .

THERE DOES NOT SEEM to be any strength like that strength which comes to a person who is forced to stand alone.

HOW CAN YOUNG MEN in their 20's — barely world-exposed — write with such flash and certitude about life when I am still nothing but confusion, an open-mouthed and goggle-eyed questioneer transfixed by the complexity of so many problems and so many possibilities? How can they say precisely what *is* when the only apparent rule of life is change, the constant converting of what *is* into what *isn't* any more? My puzzlement has been, and remains: how can strong attitudes towards life's fundamental problems be achieved — not only at an early age but ever (. . . We will pause here to allow those in the wings who are mentally drumming their fingers and rolling their eyeballs heavenward in restrained impatience to say in quiet tones: "Wadsworth, strong attitudes are simply those beliefs held by strong selves. The person with the strong self knows, instinctively or from reason, that almost any belief will satisfy and thus be counted 'strong' if there is simply a self for it to be attached to. Neither the person with a full stomach nor the person with an empty one gets neurotic in a supermarket looking at the thousands of cans of food to choose from; it's the person with no stomach at all who panics").

My point, regardless of how neurotic it is, is this: for every attitude held there are 25 others in varying angles of oppositioin, all maintained vigorously by men of superior mind (both healthy and neurotic). Obviously, a synthesis of them, as they are put forth and maintained, is impossible. So what are you, the Hamletized, to do in order to become Alexander? You are supposed to do the thing that is considered the earmark of both foolish youth and jut-jawed maturity: you reject the pressures and counsels and proclaimed wisdoms of others and do — or believe — what *you*, personally, want to do or believe. In a youth, this is referred to as behaving in a "headstrong manner": he will not listen to the "accumulated wisdom of the ages." In a man of increased years, this very behavior is said to constitute maturity and is the hard core necessary for personal integrity, courage, manhood, and greatness: "He does not straddle fences; he will take sides, even if he ends up being gloriously and stubbornly wrong;" or "They said it couldn't be done, but ———— did it;" or "Be sure you're right, then go ahead." So Davy Crockett went ahead to the Alamo, and Hitler to kill the Jews.

Thus we have it: strong personal attitudes towards what is

considered fundamental in life. The Mohammedan, the Baptist, the Catholic, the Segregationist — all are convinced they are right; just as many believe they are wrong. But all hold their positions strongly and are given that highest accolade: they are *men.*

HILL COUNTRY TOWN at night: Hands, arms, worn blue oilcloth — they were partially visible in the yellow square of a kitchen window as I walked by in the street. Vines grew around the window, framing it. A dog was barking in the yard. Someone coughed on the dark front porch. I walked on.

It was just a little past nine o'clock. The town was quiet, adjusting to summertime dark.

On another block another house: huge, silent, looming, empty. Crickets made peaceful sounds from the picket fence weeds; there was a high singing from tree frogs in the hackberry trees.

Down the street a boy was slanting through a vacant lot. He fired his BB gun twice into the shadows, waited a moment, fired once more, then disappeared.

A porchlight burned at a corner house. Beneath the light a pair of old man's shoes sat in a wooden swing.

I walked, finally, to the edge of town, where the narrow, unpaved street went off into country darkness. In a grassy lot a long wooden building waited behind its faded sign for travelers who seldom came any more. Passing under a single naked bulb that lit up the sidewalk sign — HOTEL — I shifted my suitcase to the other hand and went inside.

I AM STUCK HERE in the middle of eternity and I don't know what to do about it.

THE HILL COUNTRY on a summer day: the lazy, hazy sense of rich heat. Houses and roads and summer boys' camps are stuck here and there in the earth like currants in a rich pudding. Everywhere there is the pleasant, unobstrusive handiwork of people — gateposts, barns, by-passed bridges left from simpler times.

I DON'T HAVE anything big to say so I go around trying to crack open atoms.

GROWING UP THE 1930's and '40s, I was accompanied in the afternoons by a friend that I assumed was permanently fixed in the world. This was the sound of the small, propeller-driven airplane that was always making its slow droning way across the sky. There it was in the background, as much a part of the earth's vocality as the crow of a rooster or a train whistle in the distance or a sheep bleating in a pasture. It was not the disruptive and awesomely centralized noise that today's jet aircraft is. Why, when you heard the hum of a propellered plane it was almost like the sound of God—genially become manifest in a afternoon yawn. . . .

AGED WOMEN in wheel chairs: they are rolled along hospital corridors like prehistoric animals being transferred to a museum after at last becoming extinct.

WRITING AS VOCAL EXPRESSION: letting your inner voice finally possess its own sound, letting it speak naturally, with the richness of its own throat, Not the mind composing, carefully putting together; not an act of intelligence. Instead, the personal sound of one who, having experienced a certain flow and cadence in life, wants to tell of it, wants to dignify that flow and cadence through human speech.

THE LAND GIVES PEOPLE who live close to it a certain innocence and grace.

THE YOUNG MAN sat down at the counter and waited. He was not at ease. When the waitress came over to take his order, he waggled his jaw, twisted his shoulders, shifted himself about on the stool, yawned — all just in order to say that he wanted a hamburger and some French fried potatoes.
You see, the young man was suffering from a crisis of self. That

unsure body and mind of his had suddenly been confronted by a pretty and efficient Mexican girl in an apron, and he, country boy from Bandera, Texas, was obligated to state his need. He, Darrell Crenshaw, aged 17, 178 pounds, had to exhibit his face, his voice, his body, his clothes, his acne — all that he conceived of as being *him* — and he had to listen to himself as he did it.

And he just wasn't up to it. It was too much of a strain.

I AM HAUNTED by life — is that possible?

RAVINE AT DUSK: small birds in a brush pile, fussing, moving down among the branches into the damp, fallen leaves. . . . And unseen cows lifting muzzles in the light mist and screaming long-throated sounds into the darkening pastures. . . . Sundown, and the smell of cool air, wet wood, rocks and earth.

I AM NO ONE. I am an osmotic membrane pulsing between the lives of other people. I am a screen on which events are shown.

I WONDER if all that is good finally, in the showdown, is a big expression of yourself, when you have gone in with your hands and scooped out your insides and held them hot and steaming to the world, as an offering.

IT IS A TERRIBLE THING trying to sit still long enough to listen to life, to feel out its crevices and call them by all their rightful names.

ONE EITHER FONDLES his loved one — with tenderness, with infinite care, with that overflowing that is within him — or he fondles something else, a substitute. How much of my writing — and of others — is real creative urgency and how much is the simple fondling of a thought, an idea, a scene, a remembrance? How much of writing is sublimation?

BOTH BEATIFIC CONTEMPLATION and ruddy human life are my gods, but I am not devout enough to worship either at length.

I DON'T EVER WANT to fall in love again — not as I have before. In love I am abject, a worshipper of my loved one and a negator of my self. I pour out everything and save nothing.

I want to release love, yes. I want to flood its tenderness on another and feel the melting deep inside me and the constant outgoing surge. But I don't want it to consume me. I want to love and still retain my soul.

WHERE TO START, in describing the rage of one not able to live contentedly with himself but who knows that he must strike some sort of truce with himself or disintegrate. There is this constant war, this constant dissatisfaction which lies on my thoughts like old bacon grease on clear spring water: I seem not to be on my way any place; I have accomplished no real job yet.

I write words with the tired directedness of a person about to be conscripted for some lengthy service (even my teeth are set hard against each other, though now and then I feel obligated to raise them apart, as a small gesture toward good mental health).

Perhaps there should arise a school of writing premised on the idea that a tired or despairing mind creates with more impact than a fresh and therefore capricious one. The despairing mind is one-tracked, dogged, wholly self-contained; and though it only peers down its one long dark tunnel, the small image at the end is sharp and clear and undeniable. Such a mind is like a stripped-down, tough little fighter: it is in no mood to take any crap, is anxious to get the bout over with, and though not equipped with a boxer's skill or finesse, perhaps, it is nevertheless supplied with the grit and power of an aroused personal morality.

Daily despair and belittlement — that is the real and private reward of one desperate with desire to find what it is he should be doing and doing well. Bursting, he attempts to contain himself even more (— he doesn't know where to burst to, and mere senseless bursting, while possibly therauputic, fails to solve the chronic despair).

THERE ARE PLACES in the hill country — river places — that stay in my mind like love affairs, and on hot city days I think of them: I remember the delights of river rocks and river air; I remember river-bendings and river spaciousness.

There is a stretch of the Llano, up above Harper, where the rock bed of the old river is wide and flat; where water moves down the center in a bare shallow stream, dropping here and there into pleasant little pools; where bluffs rise on either side to remind you of the way the river used to be in the giant, silent times of eons past.

The place is called Cedar Springs, and during the summer ranch families go there in the late afternoon to spread checkered table cloths near the spring and eat supper as the sun goes down.

You can still go there, in the heat of the day, and wade barefooted in the narrow rock-bottomed stream. You stand there, minnows waiting near your toes, and you look up and down the wide river bed. You see its wet places and weeds, the easy sweep southward as it curves out of sight, the sky and the light and the trees on the bank. You stand bareheaded on the rock floor of the Llano, in July, in the sun, with willows nearby, and a spring, and shade. You stand very still, feeling the presence of this river place — its silence and heat, its beauty, its earth-godliness — and you feel like a saint.

WHAT'S *he* DOING?
"Oh, he's in there puzzling out life."
Brief snicker.

ART, psychiatry: trying to *get rid of* past experiences?

MEMORY ALONE ENRAPTURES. You find yourself, periodically, clawing back into its reaches like someone possessed of a vague but persistent hunger.

This is a great game and a lasting one: searching backward for the best hidden crystals of your experience. Your past is all inside you like pressured geological ages, and somewhere, you feel, are the gems of yourself in forgotten Mother Lodes. The challenge is to search down the hall of darkened mirrors — down past the broken, familiar relics — and without becoming overly bruised or lost come upon the outline of your many-layered Troy.

YOU CANNOT HONESTLY explore *with* someone. All observation is personal. An impulse, an insight cannot be shared.

THE SONG OF AFTERNOON: I have long wanted to sing it but I could never learn the words, or even the proper melody. I have listened hard, let my senses drift over the land and touch carefully the things that were there; I have let them bring back their findings. But all I end up with are elusive fragments, snatches of intimacy:

a herd of undisturbed red cows eating their way beyond the shade of oak trees into the lessening heat and the finally shadowing grass

the swift movement of flies as they pass in continual self-concern

a mockingbird high on a telephone pole, revolving the many sounds in his throat like a flamboyant aristocrat

small sparrows hidden deeply inside their lower-middle-class nests: carefree, talkative, unworried, and loving it

mesquite trees, radiantly shining in the sunlight like pale-green female flames: frozen in the peaceful air and no longer burning

*oaks — the constant enigma of hill country afternoons: having
such great dark trunks and giving off so much deep permanent
shade (— with scattered brown leaves of the oaks down in the
grass, smiling back toward the lowering sun like the golden faces
of blind, good-natured boys)*

*and always an inevitable thing: that sloping away of a mound
of grass underneath a tree, with limb shadows striped and angled
across it: that simple, beautiful, meaningless puzzle still lingering
unsolved from childhood — spread out, unchanged, for another
long gaze.*

I HAVE NO VISION.

I believe I have the willingness to work hard, the ability to express a thought with clearness, an untiring hunger for truth, the necessary sense of world mystery, the tempering compassion for things around me, the eye for the revealing detail, the compulsion to endlessly observe, and the desire and impulse to be honest above all else.

But I have no vision.

My gun is loaded but for the life of me I cannot spot a target I want to shoot. There is nothing that causes me to leap into the writer's saddle and ride like a crazed and fearless cossack across the steppes of my fictional Fatherland.

IN MY CONSTANT self-analysis I have become that doctor in the Virgil Partch cartoon who, with his shirt off and the stethoscope pressed against his own chest, instructs himself: "Now cough."

I SANG "GREEN EYES" loudly to several Hereford cows while the camp coffee bubbled on the open fire and the wind moved steadily across the beautifully thick winter grass.

IT'S GOT TO BE MY WAY — with my eyes and my body —

or it will never be any good. Now, if I only had a "way" that I could believe in, I would work at it joyfully.

To STOP FOR A BEER in post oak country, at Christmastime: to notice the roadside beer joint ahead, to slow down, to pull off the highway onto the shiny, rounded, reddish rocks and hear them grind comfortably underneath the tires; to stop; to open the beer joint door and hear the loose, jangling sound of the bell as you enter; to buy a beer and come outside and take the first cold sip from the can; to watch a car approach down the highway, see it pass, hear it finally disappear; to look across the road and see the many bare post oaks beyond the fence; to drink again from the cold can; to continue to stand there on the smooth reddish rocks, listening to the silence of a winter afternoon as other cars go by; to remain there, paused, and to feel how it is to be inside the day, your life, a single moment.

WE ARE SHAPED by the vacant moments of childhood. . . .
Paused at a San Antonio street corner, waiting with his parents for a street light to change, a boy listens to car horns in the downtown traffic. As he watches people moving by on the sidewalk he forms large, fundamental impressions about life. (He will spend the rest of his day reacting to a face in a clothing store, a glint of sun on a car's blue fender.)
Yet it is all perceived peripherally, almost unconsciously, as the boy stands there in the glaring midday light, waiting to cross Houston Street to buy a pair of tennis shoes.

I'VE NEVER BEEN WILLING to settle for a *useful productivity*. I seem to be always holding out for some blazing revelation of my immortal significance.
I have had no truck with the merely competent or even the fairly good — as far as my writing goes. No faint praises for me. Masterpiece or failure: I'm polarized to demand one or the other.

AFTER WORKING HOURS, after duties are through, my temperature drops to a low simmer. I buy razor blades or a movie ticket with a heavy constrained politeness, with an exceedingly deceptive mannerliness. I cause no fuss. There is not the least flare of surface emotion. I hardly impinge on my surroundings and I just barely occupy space. I am barely matter. I am a thin cardboard cut-out of a human being.

Yet behind this cardboard mask a huge furnace heats bucket after bucket of molten emotions, each ready to be tipped at an instant's notice. It is as though a wall of asbestos separates the external, public me, with my sustained low heat and apparent lack of radiation, from the inner purgatory me, where wild shapes flicker on my furnace wall and steadily bubbling buckets are covered with the magnesium-bright foam of undirected desire.

I'M ALMOST GETTING to feel unwholesome.

IT SEEMS THAT a God could not have constructed human creatures needing more desperately the very things which are denied them.

SINCE THERE ARE few fashions in nature, the men who live close to the land tend to resist change. They know that corn is planted, goats are sheared, peaches are picked, hogs are butchered — all at the proper time each year. There are few innovations, few demands for change, simply because there are not very many ways that country people can ignore the cycles of nature and still make a living. Thus rural living remains the same — always based on traditions, always conservative.

TEN O'CLOCK, and another April morning has found its harmony. No mismovements of wind, no exaggeration of sun or clouds. Greenery, buildings, sky — all are in tune and having their proper voice in how to run the early hours. Shadows, slanting sharp and firm across the ground, have begun to assert themselves:

"Look at us," they boast, "look at our weight and structure. We are the strong black ribs of the day." And the air — it is poking about, nudging tall grasses along vacant lots and the loose neckties of men talking on street corners (spring air: God's invisible cosmetic, adding emphasis).

IF YOU'RE A WRITER, you will write. If you are not, you won't. It's as simple and complex as that. You may fret and worry and self-doubt yourself all over the place, may try and abort, may start over again and despair and give up, eyeing the words jaundicedly, then creep back once more. It's the nature of the game. But if you're a writer, good or bad, you won't ever give up trying to write and won't stop thinking about writing. It will possess you — *it* being some vast, partly unseen and unknown feeling about life. It always seems so huge and just-around-the-corner that you feel inadequate for the job; you believe that you don't think big enough or clearly enough.

But if you are a writer, you will keep on trying despite yourself, despite everything that is reasonable and safe and evident. It will cause many afternoons and nights of inner fury and self-contempt and missteps. But somewhere along the way the cement of desire will begin to mix with the elusive vapors of experience, and you will begin making something solid. You will sense — suddenly and joyfully—that you can do it, that you can and must write.

AM I OVER THAT FIRST WAVE of self-pity which promotes amateurism?

IT WAS AS IF some vital spiritual organ deep inside me was slowly atrophying, and I was crying out for some revitalizing chemistry to save it.

THE TIME WAS the '30s and the town was Center Point, where the Harlesses lived in the dark rooms of their unpainted frame house.

When we went to visit them we turned off the San Antonio highway and went down the slope to the Guadalupe River crossing — I would listen to the tires change their hum as we drove over the low-water bridge — and then we climbed to the opposite side and were in Center Point. It was Sunday and the streets were quiet — although Center Point was so small and by-passed and full of shade trees and old people that the town always seemed like Sunday to me, no matter when we went. We drove slowly past small wooden houses and small yards full of flowers, and when we got to the Harless place we parked by the fence in the shade of a chinaberry tree. We looked once toward the house, then got out and walked toward the front yard gate.

(Yet there was more to it than that, for the ordinary slamming of our car door, in the silence of Sunday noon, sounded like a thunderclap before a storm. It was as if the trees and grass of the yard, the vine-tangled porch, the old couple poised like museum dummies inside the museum-like house — it was as if they had been waiting all morning long for that one sudden sound, had been dozing within Center Point timelessness until the shutting of the car door abruptly announced: Sunday visitors; time to come alive.)

Mother, Daddy, and I would go inside the Harless house and there they were, the two of them: a very old, very small, white-haired woman, her hair parted in the middle and pulled behind her neck in a bun: a barely-able-to-move old woman, coming toward us like a slow-motion swimmer through the deep-sea shadows of the living room; and a very old man, in his nineties, with black moles on his forehead and cheeks, tall and bald-headed except for a fringe of very white, very fine hair above his ears: a bony old man dressed in black, almost invisible to us except for the shining whiteness of his hair.

Mother would take Mrs. Harless by the arm and guide her carefully back to the screened-in side porch. They would sit at an oil cloth-covered table in the center of the porch and shell the rest of Mrs. Harless' garden peas while they talked. Daddy and Mr.

Harless would continue to stand there in the living room — Mr. Harless looking as if he were not aware that he was standing at all, as if he had forgotten where his body was after he had risen from his chair to greet us.

Finally Daddy would suggest that it might be cooler if they sat on the front porch. Mr. Harless would open his mouth and his jaws would begin to quiver a little and he would manage to say it: *yes*: the word strange and distant and hollow and fragile, sounding as if someone were talking through a very long rusty pipe. Then with Daddy holding the door open, Mr. Harless would shuffle out onto the porch. They would sit there on the smooth wooden bench, looking toward the deep greenery of the yard through the deeper greenery of the vines.

For a while I would look at the walking canes hanging by the fireplace on pegs, at the old photographs in their oval, glassed-in frames. But I did not want to stay inside the house; there was too much darkness, too much that was old and faded. A dim hallway went down the center of the house, with a bucket of well water on a stand silhouetted by the back yard light at the other end. I would get a drink from the dipper and then wander outside to stand under the chinaberries.

The Harless house was the only one I had ever visited that rested on small posts, that was completely open underneath. I would sit on a stump and watch the huge gray-and-white domi-necker chickens walking around underneath the house — half naked from molting, fluffing themselves in the gloomy dust.

I WANT TO WRITE good things so badly that I subconsciously believe that desire alone will compensate for the short-coming which I have. Endure, I tell myself, and perhaps that will be better after all. Endure and be honest, and maybe that will be better in the long run than genius or great talent.

Yet I hate to think I am just a pale and prideful copy of a real writer.

IT IS BETTER — or so goes the party line — to believe that black is white and that roosters are sprung from green cheese than to hold to no belief at all. To the average man there is something unclean and even dangerous about the person who isn't ready either to denounce a thing with a curse or clasp it to his chest with hearty praise. The world respects a partisan, though it may not love him.

I STRUGGLE MANFULLY to think important thoughts and always have to be content merely to think my own.

LET ME BE a celebrant of things, not their mere recounter. Let my word-attempt be able to rise of its own spirit and ascend before your mind's eye to some place *out there,* above you, fixed onto space by its truth for you and for itself. Let my words serve as guides for your own eyes, and perhaps teach them where to look and how to see. Let them, like music, take you from that place where you are and show you where it is possible to be.

I LIKE SHEEP. I'm one of their few champions. But just *look* at them sometime — maybe when it's the heat of the day and they are bedded down underneath a big liveoak, all bright-eyed and waiting for the sun to go down. They are like a massed meeting of retired simpletons, gathered to hear a speech by Ike Eisenhower.

A BORE WITH A HIGH I.Q.: she went around espousing her intelligence as if it were a cause or ideology.

I WAS ON A HILL this afternoon, before the sun went down. A valley was spread before me. And as I watched, the old feeling for the land rose inside me. As always, it was a strange excitement, a trembling exaltation and passion. It spread through me like some weakening Oriental potion (". . . ah, this eventide once more, when the country gods are here about me and I am one with Buddha. . .").

It is a simple contentment, the only consistently profound moment I have ever known. It says, among other things, that the world is good and right just as it is. It makes you think of God. It makes you lose your sense of discrimination, makes you love each thing you see — each touch of breeze on grass, each small bell sound from sheep in the valley, each frozen-neck lizard staring at you from his rock.

You love from the inside of your body. You sit there and glow.

I have asked myself many times: why this solitary bliss, these moments that melt you and spread through you this powerful mixture of melancholy and joy? These passing moments — are they what you had in your childhood but have lost along the way? In those long momentous years as a child, did you create some voice of your deepest self that cries out now to be heard? Did you create some Babylon of solitary happiness which you will never possess again but which you must keep on hunting because it seems to be on the very edge of truth, of peace, of understanding?

WAITRESS: She carried beer to the tables, her strapless sandals popping against calloused bare heels. Her breasts, once large, were fallen now, but they did not sag or bounce very much within her T-shirt: the brassiere held them, though not enough to salvage their former watermelon glory. Her full Spanish skirt flared and billowed as she walked; it hinted that the air gathered within its folds was a kind of sensual fluid in which her legs enjoyed moving on warm afternoons. Her arms, with their stringy muscles showing beneath the skin in suggestive undercurrents, were shiny and soft with age — the very smoothness seeming to tell of many abrassive caresses once given by old beaus.

I THINK I COULD lay down my life for certain frame houses

I come across just at dusk: ones held in that special last light the earth gives itself moments before dark.

. . . Just a common frame house, without fence or walks or much of anything at all; merely painted and shingle-roofed and set back a little way from the road. There are trees nearby, of course, with the locusts in them beginning to whir.

Lights off, doors shut, people gone — a house gathering darkness within its porch and eaves. A house sitting there, patiently, with only its front windows seeming alive: with the headlights of occasionally passing cars beginning to play like faint streaks of lightning across the panes.

FOR THE PAST several years it seems that I have been going more and more underground. Finally all that is going to be left of my original self will be an aroma.

WHAT IS WILL and Will Power? What is Thought and then what is Preoccupation? What is Sentimentality and what is Compassion? What is Openmindedness and what is Indecision? What is Right Action? When do you Throw It Up As A Bad Job, and when do you See It Through? And what is the satisfactory answer to Sex in the Unmarried State?

LIFE HAS GONE FLABBY, and I am flabby too. Where are the dynamics that once made a thing important, that once gave an event its color and thrill and meaning? I live on a long, gray plateau, stretching out of sight. How did I get here? How did I arrive at this spongy and weary plain, this old man's dull savannah? Am I destined to measure it, semi-serene (as a bright-eyed vegetable might be semi-serene), semi-alive, semi-myself? I keep looking around for chains to shake off or adversaries to confront or contingents to ally myself with. But no. It's merely this long gray day, this low-pulsed world I never wanted. A constant pale vista.

MOST PEOPLE never look *at* an object; they look *toward* it.

LET'S SAY I WANT to know what a building "is." So I proceed to destroy it, trying to find its vital innards and its secret. But after I destroy it, it "isn't" any more. What the building "was" turned out to be nothing. A building is only a building when it *is* a building.

Is this what was meant by a rose is a rose is a rose? Is there never any real answer or secret to a thing? Is a thing, as it exists, its own and only answer? Does a fierce desire to *know* ultimately lead to destruction, not knowledge?

BEAUTY IS THE ABSENCE of power. A person who consciously tries to make beauty does so because there is no urgency to the force within him. Beauty is an echo of the power he cannot summon forth but can only hear.

A MOMENT REMEMBERED: A male vocalist's voice echoing through a high school gym, filtering through the constant swirl of shuffling feet and colored lights: Frank Sinatra, '42, singing "All or Nothing at All.". . . then the chilling, sweet, impersonal trumpets taking over, burying the vocalist's voice in the pure crushed ice of their unisoned sound.

A PLACE JUST OFF the Harper Road: A woman works in her garden, hoeing in her row of beans. She has a bonnet on even though it is late summer and the sun is mild.

There are oak trees around the yard; the lots in back are well-kept. In front of the house, beside the cattleguard, Johnson grass grows high in a shallow ditch.

A place just off the Harper Road. . . . That's how you would refer to it in the hill country. The Old Karger Home. Years ago it was called the Old Hopf Ranch. German names on the mailboxes; hard-working people on the land. . . .

The children have grown up and left for jobs and marriage. The husband, after years of steady work, is dead. The woman, in her seventies, is by herself on the ranch now except for a hired hand.

Yet at six o'clock on this August afternoon there is no air of sorrow or loneliness about the place. The garden is green, the cows are fat, the fenceline is still durable and in good repair. As the mild sun pours in from the west the woman works steadily in her rows, her back arced in its strong, accustomed curve. A border collie lies in the shade of a pecan tree, watching as the woman digs.

TRUTH IS ALWAYS the residue left in the bottom of the barrel of experience. You never reach it in time, and it is never quite enough to matter.

DALLAS HAS A VOICE which seems to say: Adapt to us. We are generally correct about things. Whereas Fort Worth is open, toneless. It says, Well, whatever it was that people brought with them, they've probably still got. You roll your own here. . . .

Fort Worth — drab, disheartened, disheartening; not truly caring too much. Dallas — confident; a well-heeled bully.

POOR LITTLE RICH DOG: I was passing by a fine large house with many trees and winding walks when I happened to notice a Pekinese barking into a high shrub. Although I stopped and waited to see if something would come out — a cat or squirrel or maybe even a small boy — I didn't really expect anything at all to appear. And of course nothing did. The dog was obviously much too anxious in his barking. His little cries were too petulant, each one broken off sharply as he raised his muzzle skyward and then dragged it to the side. Nothing was ever going to come out; he just *wanted* something in the bushes.

There it was: a great house with a rolling lawn and luxuriant trees, but nothing at all in its bushes. Hedges sculptured and grass trimmed to a precisioned edge, but nothing for a laundried and tidied little Pekinese to be a dog for.

He would bark fitfully, then stop and stand with his legs apart, as if listening to himself, as if saying, "Well, I *could* bark pretty good at something if it would ever show up."

I left him there — practicing, and hopefully waiting.

THE OTHER NIGHT I walked past a car and saw a little boy standing in the front seat beside his mother. He had on a pair of brown corduroy overalls that crossed in the back and fastened on two dark brown buttons in front. He was standing next to the steering wheel, watching the door of a grocery store through the windshield.

How I would have liked to be that father when he came back to the car with the groceries: to have opened the door and handed the sack across to my wife and then got in and received the hug that my son had been saving for me: to have felt those corduroy pants and soft flannel shirt against my face and those two arms going around my neck and tightening.

SINCE THE WORLD is not a petty or shoddy thing, I don't want to *write* a petty or shoddy thing; I feel I would be letting the world down.

IF I MOVED WITHIN a literary circle, someone would have long ago pronounced: "Bode thinks he can take a few trees and a little silence, add a dash of self-pity, mix well with late afternoon or night, and come up with something called Life. But he never writes about Life; he just keeps on drawing his own portrait and playing Little Boy Lost as mood music, Gordon Jenkins-style."

MY WRITING IS a puzzled striving toward the most intimate thing I know.

IT SEEMS THAT my life has become a matter of operating a strange cannon which appeared, complete with concrete emplacement and body straps, several years ago. The main feature of the cannon is that it can be cranked by hand to point both below and above the horizon. So each day I get up, go to the emplacement, strap myself in place like the good conscientious gunner I am, and proceed to mow down my earthly targets with the steady dedication of a white leghorn mechanically pecking away at bits of rock and corn.

But when the end of the day comes — ah, how eagerly I change calibrations and crank my barrel to point toward the heavens. Now *that's* where the *importants* targets are! That's where you aim if you are going to be a metaphysical Sergeant York. That's the real battleground.

But there has never been anything to shoot up there — a cloud, a lost duck, maybe a few sun rays. Seldom more. I sit there, just as carefully strapped in as during the low-horizon hours, anxious to fire, restless to blast away at something worthwhile. But I see nothing, always nothing. And late at night — cold, hungry, disillusioned — I must crank the barrel down again to point below the trees: to point, like the white leghorn's beak, at the next morning's bounty of rocks and grain.

I HAVE BECOME like a watchful paramecium: flowing from one situation to another, ingesting, absorbing.

HIDING within me is significance. (Hiding within me is *me*).

GARNER PARK: A May afternoon in, say, 1949 — high school graduation day — and young couples in bathing suits dancing on the terrace of the park cafe to Buddy Clark's "Linda" and Artie Shaw's "Summit Ridge Drive."

Polished-oak doors and posts gleaming from the shadows of stone-arched passageways; bubbles circling through the red neon of the nickelodeon; couples sitting hand in hand on the low flagstone wall.

Tall trees and shadows, pleasant sunshine, the Frio River running cold and blue at the foot of the bluff — and high school seniors happily unaware of the years ahead.

AT NIGHT near SMU even the crickets seem upper middle class. (how would crickets sound in Johannesburg?)

IF I FIND or create a meaning, a destiny, a purpose for my life — that is, a work to do — will I automatically find meaning in and for the world, since the world will thereby contain my work?

Microcosm reflecting macrocosm — is this the key to understanding life and finding peace within it? Everything big in life rooted in, reflected by, everything small? ("I got the whole wide world, in mah hands. . . ."?) Look into the atom and, peekaboo, there's the cosmos staring back at you?

SHOULDERS, the spread wings of masculinity's great virile bird.

HOW PEOPLE LIKE to say "Bethesda." "We're going to Bethesda. Johnny-my-husband is working in the (place impressive name here)." How connotatively rich the name is: the great center of set-jawed dedicated men of science in the great enlightened East. How casually it is used to de-stature anyone who is not going there for a stint.

I FIGHT YOU and yet love your power, you damned *word.*

WHAT *is* A WORD? a distillation of thought and feeling guided into print under the quiet distant eye of yourself, and then promptly calculated for its effect.

NATURE HIKE REMEMBERED: We walked along the trail toward the firing range and then moved up higher along the side of the hill behind camp. We could hear the crack of the rifles below us and see part of the firing range shed through the tops of the Spanish oaks.

I had seven boys in my nature study class, and they tried to identify trees and shrubs as we walked along. (They liked the agarita bushes with their red berries and sharp-pointed leaves, and the mullen plants: I pulled off their big hairy leaves and explained that people used to smoke them like tobacco.) A couple of boys who were carrying jars would turn over logs and see what they could find underneath. We examined gray and green splotches of lichen growing on big rocks. We hunted for arrowheads.

It was warm at ten o'clock and the boys soon had sweat under their eyes. We took rest stops in the shade and looked out at the morning and the pleasant greenery of the trees. A cardinal sailed into a clearing with a sudden flash of red; there was the smell of leaves and cedar bark and rocks and dirt. Doves would call from far away and whenever they stopped we felt the silence of the rocky hillside.

We climbed to the top of the hill and walked along the horse-path. There were many cedar trees and patches of yellow June flowers. A breeze would blow now and then, making the yellow flowers wobble, and there would be an easy moving of the papery Spanish oak leaves above us. Huge flint rocks lay out in the sun like bronze, rounded animals, and buzzards drifted high above us, and somewhere in the valley below a hawk kept screaming.

IT IS FANCY I try to shape. I try somehow to get above the thing in mind and then squint down with a half-closed eye at the promising angles of possibility. . . . Thank you, but no cooking up of credible realisms for me: it is the dishing out of words and thought within my own personalized broth that I value. Perhaps this is anti-art, a denial of the sweat of fiction's discipline. So be it. Instead of fictioneer I will be word musketeer, using my sword of speculation to impale the varied morsels of happenstance.

(for there is some kind of rhythm in me, a private psalmody, and it very much shapes the issue here. I seem to need, and want, ballbearings in my print. I can't write of late without an inclination to swing the lines, instintively choosing only those words to say which suit a certain lilt and music in my thought

(is it some rather simple urgency I follow in this — the gathering together of wandering words to fit the idle tap of my minstrel-foot? Am I Jungle Boy with a two-stringed harp, trying to assuage with a little harmony the loneliness of my congo-dark?)

I LOVE THE RANCH — the ranchhouse itself, primarily, and its yards, but also the lots and fields, the pastures that go to the horizons with trees and varied risings of land, the seasons that come and go and the animals and birds that remain. The ranch means my grandparents who have lived there for over half a century. It means good morning breezes, and wasps crawling into the mouths of front yard hydrants, and windmills turning, and boards weathering. It means the smell of homemade pillow cases and the feel of cool kitchen linoleum against your bare feet on late summer nights.

The ranch is a near-completeness, a near-perfection; it allows for human living at an unneurotic pace. It is what the body of a woman is to a man, a church is to one devout. It is uncomplicated peace.

I HAVE A MEMORY: the feed store just after sundown. Daddy and I are getting into the cab of the pickup and starting home. It is a cold winter night, with dust above the unpaved, rocky streets; through the dust and cold I can see the warm, round, friendly-looking brake lights of the cars in front.

Everything in the memory is good: the just-after-darkness, the hanging caliche dust, the chilled air and worn truck-metal doors of the cab, the sense of mutual purpose — of everyone going toward warm houses where yellow lights shine through the trees. And the feeling of being a boy in a pickup beside the person who was your father — of riding the same streets with other men in other trucks and cars that were bouncing homeward through streets full of darkness and gasoline smells and brief glares of headlights and reflections from neon signs: that was perhaps best of all. It was a sense of community-at-dusk; a feeling of being sharers in winter-night rituals. . . .

AND THERE IS this memory, too: the day I went to Center Point with Daddy to deliver feed. It was mainly the sacks themselves I recall — those fine, full sacks of maize, fifteen or so, a pickup load.

I was ten or eleven, and because I was beginning to form certain vague but general attitudes toward life maybe it seemed, somehow, a proper thing that we were doing: *dealing in grain.* And maybe it struck me, obliquely but strongly, that it was good to be out in the day, as we were, so that you could see the countryside — the farm buildings here and there, the trees, the highway in the sun, the *openness* of the afternoon. Maybe I just liked the casual work routine of being with Daddy in the cab of the pickup, stopping finally near Center Point and unloading the nice-looking, nice-feeling sacks from the back of the truck.

As I recall the mood of that day, it was like being inside one of those illustrations in a child's first reader: Farmer Brown's place, with red barns and railing fences and friendly sun and ultra-green trees. Perhaps I was a small Van Gogh, responding to radiant sunflowers and roadside air.

EACH DAY I see her, round-eyed, round-faced, smiling, leaning sideways from her row like an orange-topped sucker sticking from a jar of candies. Perhaps I dreamily attempt some humorous remark — and immediately consider it lost on my pleasant but inert jawbreaker class — when I hear Lorenda's laugh, that low flat cackle, and I look up to see her lollipop face with half-moon grin and small raisin eyes. The sound of the laugh is a soft, even *heh-heh-heh,* an essentially un-girl-like sound, and each time that I hear it I think of a George Pal puppet leaning suddenly around a haystack and cracking a smile. For she is exactly that: a living cartoon, a merry, loose-limbed little figure escaped from the pages of Pinocchio to come sit on the back row of my eighth grade English class and be amused.

WELL-POLICED, well-governed, well-entertained, industrially well-heeled, Dallas glows to itself and the outside world as a steady spark of the Civilized Southwest. It is full of sincere and earnest people. It is now a Center. It is full of Business. (But oh, let me Out.)

I TURNED MY HEAD this way and that, seeking upward into the night.

"Aha," I thought, "I'm ready this time. I feel trim inside, like an empty and ready vessel. I will turn my head in a full arc and catch the sound of the world and fill myself with its secret beauty. In my readiness, I will finally see all the hidden clarity that's been around. I will feel the touch of eternal emanations as they come striking down."

So I turned what I thought was this clear and ready surface — this suddenly poised me — and tried to let it touch like a smooth plate against the night. And for a long instant there seemed no reason why the world and I should not flow back and forth in a fluid, private dialogue, opening at last the hidden membrane of life-and-death that had stood between us. (— for during that brief moment it seemed so very possible: the world would become me and I would become it and we would finally become one. I would have reached the end of a long dedication to things Unknown).

But in the midst of that moment an earthly breeze came and touched my body — ruffling my intensity so much that its edges began to show. After a bit I had to smile at myself and move on. A foolish, questing head, cocking its ear at the universe: I might have revolved it there all night, like a scarecrow listening for symphonies in the wind.

As a sophomore in college I began standing at the corner of Sixth and Congress on Sunday mornings, not understanding why, just knowing that watching people pass by on the street was the one deeply important thing I had to do. College was nothing; the faces on the street were everything.

Even though you are unhappy, or lonely, or feeling unfulfilled, there can exist within you a saving sense of integrity, a sense of fidelity to yourself. Such a unity is the small reward for not having compromised too much along the way.

A real compromise of yourself constitutes a death somewhere in the spirit. The damage is not always immediately noticed, but it will show sooner or later. It will begin to rise up in unexpected moments, like belched gall in the mouth, and cause your very fiber to feel weakened, as though it had been left to soak in water for a long while.

And yet, there are many dire times that a reasonable person is tempted to choose a compromise rather than persist awkwardly in holding on to his almost-forgotten dreams and desires. Perhaps he has come to feel that his emotions were less than trustworthy in the past and believe that his accumulated experience has now purified and stabilized them. He is tempted to turn his back on those almost-dimmed passions which, he remembers, led so frequently to heartaches and blind alleys and failures.

So, in a state of sobriety — that is, an absence of emotion, an absence of any true desire — the reasonable person may make his compromise. He may review the long ravel of his past experience and soberly plan to circumvent any such future ravels. He may decide to accept a less-compelling vision of the world than he once had in order to consolidate whatever few gains he can recognize out of the jumble of years and deeds he calls life.

If he does, he will lose something he cannot replace. He will no longer know how it feels to have his mind and spirit in accord. Disunity will creep like ivy up his backbone. Harmony will disappear. Mind and emotions will be estranged, and will vie for leadership. Gradually the future will be robbed of glory, the past become vague and smudged, and the present sharply separated from both. Life will become a practical, day-by-day affair, lacking urgency, and our reasonable person suddenly finds himself strangely hobbled. There is no longer the old good surge, the full glad savoring, the clean springiness with which he used to meet life's best moments. There is always some oblique consideration now, some obscure dynamic to be coped with. The heart is robbed of its full throb. Glory, ecstasy, joy — these become suspect words, since the reasonable person must take care not to believe in them again. (Yet he will always be a little scared of them because he knows they did exist for him once; he knows they were valid even though they are now just wisps and hints of things he cannot catch hold of any more.)

Yes, when the man of compromise looks around him, he finds that the old feather wings of hope inside him are clipped, folded, and stored away to gather dust. Fragmented, disunified, the reasonable person will of course live on — a bit sickened but wanly and periodically smiling.

I AM mortally sad. Oh, for some companionable Platero. . . .

RANCH PEOPLE: you don't have to see them to realize they are there; you can feel their presence as you drive along the country roads. They exist on all sides in their possessions and traditions and handiwork. You pass their cattleguards, their fields and pastures, the smooth caliche roads leading from their mailboxes on the highway to their unseen homes hidden behind distant trees, and you feel, in the very air, the sense of their possession and occupation of the land.

You see where they are and what they are doing and you find yourself wanting to have a trust in them simply because they blend so well with the hard beauties of the earth.

... AN AFTERNOON SHADE in the west window, with outside light making dream-like hues of yellow around the endless whirligig movements of a shadowed chinaberry tree. A screen of constant imaginings, of wild intense golds and faint moody darks. . . . The wind blows, making the chinaberry reflections wax and wane, with stalks and leaves and vacant yellow spaces sweeping across each other in cluttered jungle scenes. Golden moons washing against each other to and fro, created and destroyed in an instant. . . .

WITHOUT LONELINESS in its deepest form I would have never been driven to write a single line. Count the words, multiply by hours, and arrive at the length and depth of my isolation.

I AM CONSTANTLY DISTURBED by the antagonisms in life, the ones that keep running like wild trains toward opposite horizons. There never seems to be any round house of Truth where the tracks finally circle back to one another so that I can finally sigh: Ahh, the confusion was mere illusion. The trains continue to thunder on within me and without, while I foolishly try to grab all possible straps for security. . . . The Silver Streak body and the Santa Fe mind: on they race through the night of human experience.

MAN KEEPS REACHING long arms into the sky, never touching the Absolutes he wants, only greater and great immensities.

THE TERRIBLE NEED to *deal* with experience, to put your knowledge and feelings to some kind of use, destroys the pleasure of living.

THERE IS A PASTURE in my life — a little stretch of flat-land beneath a hill, with oak trees and many leaves — that I carry within me as a private place. It is where I would go, I think, after a time of great despair. I would park my car and walk from the road into the woods and I would come to that spot which would not have changed since the time I had been there last. The dirt would still be richly dark under the trees, there would be leaves and grass, and if I looked I would be able to see goats grazing in the distance and maybe a few cows. I would touch the rough wood of the oaks, I would walk through the grass slowly, and I would know that I was home: I would know that the place contained an essence which was both deeply me and something deeply beyond me: something I could not identify but which I could respect, be awed by, and love.

SIMPLICITIES THAT MEAN MUCH to a child: the way lawns look in front of public buildings; the look of public buildings themselves.

I LIKE TO SINK into ordinariness, for it is out of ordinariness that perception grows.

GO SOUTH SOME AFTERNOON on the Mansfield road out of Fort Worth: that's Mississippi, except you see postoaks instead of pines and acres of rusting, junked cars instead of Negroes. Men in work hats cut across muddy yards with a wrench in their hand; they are tight-bellied and slope-shouldered and they watch you carefully, suspiciously, as you drive by. Cars are pulled up on their yellowed front yard grass; Maytags are going to rust under their chinaberry trees and on their front porches. And behind the shadowed front door screen women stand with diapered babies on their hip — looking out.

WHEN A PERSON who is content with what he has finally becomes discontent because of what others lack — that is the rare act of becoming involved with humanity. A person who does this is the only real link between the satisfied Haves and the dissatisfied Have Nots.

OF COURSE. It has been stupid of me not to realize it before now. I do have friends, and true ones. They just happen to be out of the ordinary.

A piece of paper, a bit of silence, my past — these are my companions. A lonely group we make sometimes, yes, but friends we are nevertheless.

I treat them courteously, coming into their presence with gratitude and respect. I never browbeat. I do not shake or gouge them or rattle their bones in a grim effort to draw out of them some artful tale or episode. I do not try to take advantage of them for my own possible artistic gains. I try to observe the basic rule of friendship: never to make excessive demands of those one would want to have genial concourse with over the years.

Thus, my friends and I simply sit together like old clubmen gathered together before a warm fireplace. We find a little comfort and peace from the quiet, level atmosphere, and sometimes, if the mood becomes right, there is a clearing of the throat, a shifting about in a chair, and the rising of a steady voice within the room.

I THINK of D. in college, and our long, shining spring. I think of that special quality of air, the sense of leisured afternoons, the presence of tree-shaded Austin streets. Days had the clean stereoscoptic look of washed cups hanging in a shadowed kitchen cabinet, and there was a comfortable, settled feeling to the sidewalks and lawns as D. and I walked by. Housemothers in robes watered their pot plants on two o'clock porches, city buses pulled away from shaded corners, carpenters hammered on distant roofs — and it was all very pleasant, all very pleasant indeed.

I think of sheep grazing in a field down on Sixth Street. I remember how they stood in green April grass that morning as D.

and I moved along hand in hand. They were an ordinary bunch of sheep — half a dozen or so — and even though they just inched along, heads down, eating, not bothering to look at us through the tight wire fence, they were satisfying to look at if you were college students out for a walk across town.

Maybe it was merely the idea of them more than anything else — their being there, peaceful and country-like, while trains lumbered nearby and sirens wailed and tires screeched on the hot pavement. And maybe what was important was the feeling that out of all the people in Austin that morning only D. and I understood what was good about such a small green field.

She and I saw the field, delighted in it and its methodically chewing sheep, and we knew that it helped to make us happy and contentedly alive. As we stood looking through the fence, our backs to the traffic, we understood that we were sharing this good simple thing and that it made us feel, somehow, curiously special (. . . And maybe that is what being young and in college is all about: glorying in what seem to be your own special knowledges; feeling supremely free and confident and newly aware. It is watching all the bread trucks of daily life clatter by and knowing that their burdens and duties are real enough but nevertheless feeling superior to them because they seem so passionless, so routine, so lacking in excitement and greatness and audacity and dreams.)

I think, too, of the afternoon: of borrowing my roommate's car and driving out to the lake; of D. and I walking through the grounds of Laguna Gloria for a while and then out a little peninsula, following the narrow path underneath all the tall overhanging trees; of the far end of the peninsula where we sat beside a white gazebo and looked at other pairs of college students in canoes, disappearing silently into coves; of trying to read — *Zuleika Dobson, The Magic Mountain* — but not being able to; of laying the books aside and stretching out on the grass and listening to the peacocks scream from the museum grounds while we held each other in the steaming April heat.

EVERY TRUTH is like a hurricane — a strong convincing wind with a lie hidden in the very center.

WHAT IS THE psychology of aloneness and the writer? Do you have to feel utterly alone, utterly withdrawn, before feeling sufficiently free to write, before reflection and fancy are able to invest themselves in you? Does the most minimal commitment stop up the pores of creativity? Does writing involve such a continuous inner reflection, such incessant pondering, that any sense of commitment shuts off the feeling of freedom and thus the desire to write? Does truth ever matter when you are content? Can the critical processes stay in gear when you are wholly satisfied?

(But surely there does not have to be this kind of antagonism: the writing about life, or the living of it. Surely the two can be reconciled. Surely the necessary atmosphere for writing is not aloneness forever — not always the outsider looking in.)

MANY THINGS in the world have been scorned, laughed at, belittled. But no one has ever yet ridiculed nature.

TUESDAY, FIVE-THIRTY, no place to go. Another after-work dilemma for me on the streets of Dallas.

I wait the stop lights out, driving slowly east along Gaston Avenue. I feel constricted, alone, full of vague hate.

I pass rows of new apartment buildings. In an hour or so their outside walls will be lit with dim orange glows. The secretaries are already home from work, moving about on their thick carpets in their frosted-silver hair, readying prophylactics.

I turn west on Fitzhugh, seeking relief. . . . Yes, here there are pleasant-enough houses, trees, sidewalks, and a subdued afternoon light. Such a street could make a city desirable on a fall afternoon. Yet the old dull feeling persists: that in Dallas nothing is desirable, not even life itself.

Passing a Skillern's Drug (*Skillern's, Oak Cliff,* the *Club It'll*

Do: the very names deflate you, gradually sour your mind with their bitter-almond taste), I see a Negro woman standing with a huge bundle in her arms. She is waiting for a bus. As I drive by we look into each other's face, but nothing is exchanged. We are carrying ourselves too privately; we have no room now for the space of another. . . . I wait on a red light, daydreaming. A car honks once, then shoots around me. Its radio is playing Floyd Cramer.

. . . Five-forty-five, going on six; might as well kill the twilight hours with a movie. As I park near the art-movie theater I take a look at the marquee. Another girlie movie is playing.

Walking toward the entrance I see that the small, dark-haired woman is again in the ticket booth — reading, as usual. And, as usual, I hesitate in approaching her: There she is, a woman of apparent good breeding, of sensibility, a woman who perhaps fell on hard times and was forced to take a simple-minded job; and here I am again with my dollar and a quarter, ready to gaze at Russ Meyer's amazons. I take out my wallet, a bit embarrassed, still not sure if she is one of the owners or just part-time help.

She barely looks up from her book (. . . Theodore Roethke, Beckett, Sartre?) and does not speak as she takes my money. She presses a button, a ticket appears in the small metal slot, and the woman, unsmiling, uncommunicative, returns to her reading (. . . "There he goes, another of them: straight from the office to 'Bosom Buddies'").

Inside, in the darkness, red-lipped starlets with bulging breasts move languidly through the dream life of a pop-eyed plumber in overalls. There are four of us watching from the musty seats.

When I come out, it is dark. Dallas night has been substituted for Dallas day.

I walk to the corner 7-11, buy a beer, return to my car. I drink slowly from the can, listening to the crickets in the shrubbery nearby. I am hungry, but I do not want to go to the Toddle House for a hamburger and coffee. Almost every night, it is the Toddle House for a hamburger and coffee. . . .

I lie down in the front seat and listen first to the cars passing, then to the sounds of the night. A woman walks along the sidewalk, her dog straining ahead of her on a leash. The dog stops at the car for a moment, sniffs. There is a brief silence. Perhaps he takes a leak against my door. The woman finally jerks the leash and moves on — the claws of the dog again setting up their fast little rhythm on the sidewalk.

In the quiet moment following the woman's passing I say to the darkness: Well, here we are again, just the two of us, at 8:15 on a Tuesday. In Dallas.

After a while I start the car, drive to a Toddle House, order a hamburger and coffee. I eat in silence three stools down from a man who also eats in silence. The attendant, his leg hitched up on a shelf behind the counter, stares out through the smoke of his cigarette into the nighttime traffic.

II

1962 - 1966

II

I WALK EACH NIGHT in Juarez for an hour or more, always ending up with the best-shined shoes in all Chihuahua. I walk there and keep discovering what in my childhood I had thought was life: the smell of Camphophenique in cold night air, a group of boys on bicycles gathered around a fire in an open dusty field and singing, the pale burning yellow side of an adobe building just at sundown.

I HAVE NO IDEA what a poet is, but I think he is a person who tries to peel away the thin, almost invisible tissue that camouflages all things in life and robs them of their beauty and mystery.

EL PASO IN WINTER: the exponent of beautiful days: a place where life is rich in simplicities and nothing seems ugly, somehow, not even ugliness.

It is because everything is so . . . *believable* here. Take a door at two o'clock in the afternoon: when it closes in a quiet hillside neighborhood there seems to be no place on earth where a single sound could have more right to express itself. I would walk blocks just to hear such a sound again, for it is like a judgment — verification not only of the door's existence but of my own as well.

AM I NOT SAYING that poetry is all that is worth the candle — that is, the going beyond an event to illumine it.

(for what have you got once you have learned a *fact*? A fact does not grease your anxious and straining motor, does not lead you from yourself, does not really cast a shadow. . . . So let us pray: Oh, Lord, lead me not into information.)

IN HEMINGWAY the trend toward bareness and objectivity swung to the top of its arc and then could go no further. It had to stop and swing back down in an imitation of itself. Its impetus had come from its newness, its cleansing power. But it got caught up in the greatness of its concept and could not stop; it had to exploit and perfect itself.

The author withdrew himself so hugely behind the curtain of his style that there was no sense of humanness left in the background. You read a Faulkner or Steinbeck story, and though the story moves of its own independent power you know the author is *there,* behind the words. You know that he *wrote* them, that they were not spontaneously generated or immaculately conceived. Thus you can always look up from the words and consider the author in his thoughts, even commune with him a bit.

But who could commune with Hemingway? His world is empty, as if the author-god had gone away and left his universe to spin beautifully in a meaningless orbit

(and always, that inter-line chant of: "here, weigh each of these words in the palm of your hand and find them beautiful and good and true;" always words with a too-sculptured air about them, as if they had first been put into a place by a surgeon wearing a mask and rubber gloves and then a spotlight labeled Art focused just above to illumine them properly).

SOMETIMES AT NIGHT, after walking through the streets of Juarez for a long time, I come back to sit beside the dry, dusty canal that winds through town. There, in silence, I try to puzzle out the night that stretches so hugely around me.

Sometimes I just listen to the sound of doors slamming, to the rhythm and pattern they make. They do not seem to slam at random, in complete innocence of one another, but at definite intervals. It is as though people are leaving their houses in secret scores, all following a complex, pre-arranged plan, and are silently making their separate ways to a meeting place. The night blankets their scheme so perfectly that it seems only the dogs and I know about it and understand: in the whole city, only the dogs and I are listening. And since I am used to strange things at night, to mysteries, I just sit there on the bank of the canal and listen. But the dogs — always partisans — turn their muzzles to the sky and try to warn the city, try to arouse it to the strange monkey-business going on. The city never pays them any mind and they bark long into the night, unheeded.

EMBRYOS, a quarter of an inch long, turning out to be these magnificent human creatures.

I SUPPOSE THAT an intellectual is one who always punctures the myths that most people want to live by. An ordinary man will say: Yes, such-and-such is correct — and will go away feeling pleased, glad to have no further business with the matter. Then the intellectual comes along, looks closer, and says: Hmmm, this is only 85% true — and the other 15% is not only not true but perhaps even *dangerously* false.

The intellectual is one who looks a second time — who makes the ordinary man uncomfortable by not allowing him to deal casually with truth.

I'M GETTING OUT of the habit of jobs. I think I will just keep on walking around in the afternoon: reading a little, writing a little, drinking coffee in small drugstores and cafes; *considering* things. . . .

THERE IS A LOT of writing done by the mind and body before there is a felt need to put down words. Thus it seems that a writer must be more crucible than craftsman. He can never be merely facile — that is too easy a way out; facility always comes first. A person must be willing to *wait,* must be willing to allow that stirring inside of him to grow larger, for it is that particular stirring which will not allow him to settle for anything less than the truth of emotion and thought. (Sometimes he will feel that he never consciously wrote a piece but rather allowed the thoughts and images to come boiling out of his mind of their own intensity.)

GOD IS PURE CREATION and no more. Once He has made you, He is not involved with you again until after your death. He is not someone for you to call upon, cajole, thank, expect aid from, blaspheme, or worship. He did His job — He made *you* out of *Him* — so the rest is up to you and the already-existing universe. God does not reward nor punish, become pleased or displeased. He is simply that creative force from which you came and to which you return — with the *you*, in the meantime, being that localized, particularized part of Him which He put into action at your birth. It is of no use to look for God, or cry out against God, or prostrate yourself before His spirit. For the duration of your lifetime, God is you, existing nowhere except in his creations.

SOMETIMES I FEEL like a walking indebtedness: I am kept alive moment by moment through a million courtesies of my silent body parts.

I DON'T WANT to take an easy way out and say: I'll just write sketches. Or, I'll report the hill country and its people. Or, I'll go ahead and write the standard Sensitive Boy Grows to Maturity novel. Or, I'll be diligent in my recordings and maybe someday someone somewhere will want to publish an Unknown Writer's Notebooks. No. That's not what I want: the I-don't-know-what-else-to-do approach.

FOUR BOYS in the back of a pickup, under quilts — heads popping up in the flailing morning wind, hair flying, smiling out of the boundless freedom of being young.

A PERSON CAN ONLY remain successfully sane as long as he does not perceive the true nature of the world in which he lives.

SOMETHING I HAVE DONE most of my adult life: fade out my personality almost to the zero point so that the person I am with can be more fully himself.

For it turns out there are submerged, suppressed people who will not dare show themselves in ordinary competitive relationships. They will not suffer defeat again. Only on rare occasions — when the conversational air seems still enough, safe enough — will they risk letting their ego creep out into the light. And they sometimes even get a little drunk on the headiness of knowing their own fullness once more.

WORDS ARE NOT building blocks to me; they are arrows let fly from the self.

In writing I do not want to serve any master but myself — not even the master of traditional art forms.

When I am writing the way I want to, each word hitting the page is like a piece of me jerked out of my mind and body. The typewriter key arcing forth toward the ribbon bears thought-tidings from me to the paper, to the world.

THOUGHTS-OUT-OF-THE-ORDINARY come only when you live-out-of-the-ordinary. Creativity falls asleep when seduced by comfort.

To create, to be alive, a person has to unstrap himself from the emotional safety belts of habit and routine. He must be out on the loose — thrown repeatedly upon his best resources by the unpredictable currents of his surroundings. For only a high degree of tension — indeed, anxiety — can ever stir up the thick sediments in the mind and begin to let the clear shafts of imaginative daylight come piercing through.

SOMETIMES I THINK I am too pleased by life, too satisfied by its daily simplicities. Say I am out walking on the edge of town some sunny morning—I find that all I would ever care to express about life is right there before me: the mountains lying in the distance in the early morning smoky-haze; the fields spread around me, plowed and ready for planting; the sound of tractors running and cars moving along the highway. If I wrote, I would just want to lift that whole satisfying piece of earth and sky and air and place it down on paper. So most of the time I have to ask myself: why write? You've already got what you want — *there it is,* right before you. Why not go ahead and enjoy it? Why not continue to be delighted in it and stop feeling guilty because you are unable to capture it on paper with the same skill that God used to create it?

Much of the time I follow this advice — I walk about finding pleasure and contentment just in perceiving my surroundings. Perhaps I see an old punctured oil can in a ditch. Fine, I say to myself. It exists, I exist, the two of us are here together; we have a relationship, and I am pleased by it. We are two things in life side by side — what more can you want? Or perhaps I see two women talking in a small road-side drycleaning shop. Again, fine; lovely. At such a moment I prefer seeing them — and listening to them talk — to reading Shakespeare. Or I see a sign on another building: "Ed's Welding." Also fine. I prefer looking at those black, irregular letters to seeing a play. Or, to be perfectly accurate, I had *just as soon* see the sign "Ed's Welding" as read Shakespeare or see a play. Because to me there is no hierarchy of things in life. Everything that exists is a phenomenon; everything has its own wonder. *Life* is a wonder — how, then, can anything in life not help but share part of that wonder, that mystery? To be sure, it is perhaps a matter of seeing it — like picture puzzles in childhood: a cow, for example, is camouflaged by its surroundings and you keep looking and looking and finally shrug and say, There's no cow there; and then someone points to a certain area of the picture and sure enough, staring out at you is a cow.

Most people don't find the cows in life — the everyday, ordinary phenomena. And those who do become a little paralyzed from the awesomeness of such simple delights. For if you have the right eyes, *everything* intrigues and captivates. Everything is of value simply because it *is* — it exists in the magic of its own incomprehensible being. Bums, babies, trees, filling stations, grass — all exist, and thus all are worthy of your interest, reflection, and bewilderment.

It DOES NOT TAKE any particular talent to be indifferent to others — their point of view, their rights, the dynamics of their very existence — or to follow a course of pure self-involvement. Yet it seems that those who are the most aware of other lives, other possibilities, other circumstances, are the ones least equipped for survival.

TAKE AWAY GREENERY; take away
    breeze
Take away morning; take away
    sound
Take away birds; take away
    dirt
Take away coolness, take away
    smells
Take away distance; take away
    light
    yes, take them all away, along with the morning glory vines and the weeds and the pastel Mexican houses — and bugs that crawl in the sun and bits of glass lying stuck to the ground — and then be prepared to take away me: for afterwards I will have no good reason to stay behind.

JUST LIVING: that's more than enough, any time. Living, and thinking hard as you do the living; and remembering the past, when you lived there too; and trying to put the two together — yet always finding the past hazy and strange and vaguely unreal, as if it had happened to someone very close to you but not you; and coming to feel that you are always living a bunch of separate, barely connected lives, with only childhood and boyhood approaching anything definite and real and lasting; and always wondering if that's the way it is with everyone, or just you.

WRITING IS LIKE going to a well and drawing out a bucket of strange water and pouring it on the ground. The task does not satisfy me and it has no end. I *do* it, yes, and I am left with a sense of heightened participation in a big and significant thing. But it is all to do over again. I seem to have achieved nothing, really, not even release from myself.

FIRST CHILD: It is a cool summer morning and Deborah, the baby, sits in a slanting infant seat beside a pleasantly shining mahogany door.

Outside the house little is stirring — a few casual branches of a salt cedar by the porch, a leaf or two of the young mulberries along the street.

From where I sit I can see her in the front doorway and can hear her small noises. They are very much like the sounds of the morning — melodious, periodic, peaceful. I listen first to the back-yard doves, a few neighborhood cars, a lone plane passing over the mountains; then from the living room I hear the baby shaping her broad, breathy, sighing sounds.

Occasionally there is a cool trace of air that makes its way through the open doors and windows of the house — touching the white cabinets of the kitchen, the lamps and chairs of the living room. The baby feels the air, too, and is pleased. Her small, beautifully molded legs rise together like a pair of delicate sea flowers drifting above the ocean floor; her toes move in a slow curling and stretch. As the light in the doorway shines through the edges of the toes, it pinks each one with inner halos.

After a while I go to the baby and take her from the seat and feel her small intense baby heat against my body. I stand in the doorway, the whole beautiful weight and length of her familiar flesh there in my arms, and I am empty of words.

THE TRAIN STATION: that secular temple I enter at night with praise and thanksgiving.

I AM FIT for nothing except wandering around at night and working at my words.

SINCE NO ONE ELSE wants the job, I will be the poet laureate of these city things:

Red bricks placed diagonally around front yard flower beds.
Small printed cards stuck behind fly-specked windows, announcing, without too much vigor: Apartment For Rent.
Locusts singing in tall hot elm trees at two in the afternoon.
Pipes jutting through the walls of downtown laundries, spurting steam into the tall grass of vacant lots.
Empty wine bottles lying in recessed doorways of padlocked clothing stores.
Old homes sitting naked in a block of rubble, waiting for the freeway to come on through.
Bay windows in red-brick old homes, gazing out like eyes that have gradually gone blind from the harsh glare of the twentieth century.

IF YOU WRITE as I do (that is, if you pursue writing more or less as a kind of private vice — doggedly, almost apologetically, yet all the while feeling that it is the only thing you do that is really worthwhile) then you cannot help living as I do: on an emotional knifeblade. As a Private Writer, you are like a precariously balanced human triangle, with your whole body weight supported by a single point — your words. Whether or not you stay balanced depends solely on whether the tip is made of diamond or putty.

IN THE BAR MOCTEZUMA: On Sunday afternoon Mexican women sit with their men at the long central table of the Bar

Moctezuma in Juarez, drinking beer and laughing. It seems as if they are always laughing — loudly, explosively — and even when they are not actually involved in the laughter itself their heads are rolling about from side to side in little slow, contented semicircles of enjoyment. . . . Some of the women are fat, with sweat streaks glistening in rings around their necks, and their laughs end as long shrieking screams. They slap the table with their fat hands and nudge the men with their shoulders.

It is curious about the men. On these Sunday afternoons of drinking they seem unusually polite and restrained — laughing almost formally and without their usual ease. They sit with a hand clasped about a beer bottle as though they are holding themselves firmly to a post. Most of them wear white shirts with the collars open and with the cuffs of the sleeves folded back — revealing smooth, brown hairless arms. . . . Somehow, you feel as though it is these exposed parts of themselves that cause the men to adopt their attitudes of shyness and restraint — as though the arms and hands are not really flesh at all but pieces of sleek rubber thoughtlessly left bare. Sitting decorously at the table, the men seem almost apologetic for having revealed so much of their smooth personal brownness before the ladies.

ONCE A PERSON becomes merely a hero worshipper, he ceases to behave heroically himself.

This is one of the tragedies of the South: that white men have cut themselves off from heroic action — have in fact surrendered the potential for such action to the very ones they fear the most, the Negroes. In worshipping the Lost Cause of the Confederacy they have become incapable of emulating the Confederate heroes they admire; they can now act only *un*heroically. They can only threaten or kill Negroes; can only dwell on the glories of their grandfathers; can only draw the noose of their own dilemma tighter and tighter — while at the same time refusing to let anyone come in and help them. They are impotent through too long a time of hero worshipping, and too full of rage at the Negroes' continual survival. Like all fixated men, they are dealing with the present by keeping the tightest possible grip on the past.

CHAIRS, sitting long midday hours in the harsh glare of the summer sun: How forgotten they seem, how neglected and forlorn. They look as though they have lost their souls.

Yet each night, after the sun goes down and the day softens, hands again reach out for them, readjusting them on the grass. Once again bodies sink into them gratefully and the chairs become partners in intimacy, companions in rest. . . .

WHAT A STRANGE THING it is to live. . . .

I was facing the sun on a late afternoon in June. I was looking at a row of very small, very green willows growing peaceably beside a broad sidewalk in Juarez. I saw, above the willows, a pigeon flying in a clear sky. And beyond the pigeon were shadow-dark slabs of reddish mountains.

On the other side of the walk grew a row of green elephant ears, deeply touched by the sun. I looked at them — at the same time smelling a heavy bitter scent in the air, the smell of a dog being burned on a side street, perhaps.

I could hear the sound of a jackhammer, somewhere across the river in El Paso.

The wind rose for a moment, blew against my face and against the row of small green trees. A boy walked past, barefooted, flipping a small bolt in his hand. A truck lumbered by and the boy crossed the street behind it, still flipping the bolt. The sun continued to touch brightly the six o'clock streets.

. . . I stood there and saw it all. It was called a day. And I was what is known as a human being. It and I were together, at that moment, in something called time.

Life was strong and I was in it, so I stood there, transfixed by a kind of innocence, under a deep blue sky.

SOONER OR LATER all realities become dreamlike.

ADULTHOOD: when the riot of first innocence is finally quelled.

I GUESS I HAD RATHER be in a crowd of the world's most ordinary people — in the midst of the most common human faces and flesh — than entirely alone in paradise.

YOU FINALLY ARRIVE at a fact you simply can't deny: that the world is incomprehensible. God, order, truth — such finalities may exist, but they cannot be dealt with by any of the human resources. Accepting this, what kind of daily stance do you take in order to live on? Do you simply ally yourself with recognizably human causes and ends, saying, This is all I can do or know; the rest it — the lurings of the spirit — will have to remain beyond us and our immediate concerns. Or indeed, do you keep on, doggedly, in a willful denial of all that seems sensible and reasonable, always pursuing the invisible hand that apparently set you and your kind into this terrible and beautiful human motion.

ON LATE SATURDAY AFTERNOONS, while scholars are deep in the stacks of the college library, I am down on Durazno Street with the pigeons and red-brick warehouses.

I like it there; it is a home for me.

The streets are quiet at five o'clock and the big buildings throw pleasant shadows. Mexican boys shoot baskets on a school playground. A bell jingles at a corner grocery store as Mexican girls go in to buy loaves of bread.

It is a nice little side-street community, giving the same feeling that Saturday afternoons give small central Texas towns. Old Mexican men in hats walk home carrying their sack of groceries. The pigeons move back and forth on the ledges of the warehouses. And across the railroad yard, up on the low bluff, a row of turn-of-the-century hotels and apartment houses are still in the sun, their arched windows and small green balconies and stunted palms giving them the look of a beachfront in wintertime.

I read there in my car, in front of a *ropa usada* store — looking up from time to time to watch the drifters make their slow way to the Rescue Mission in the next block. In their old worn clothes, they stand at the street corner, hand in their pockets, not knowing what step to take next on what is to them just one more colorless, toneless, empty Saturday afternoon.

WE SELDOM PAY our greatest debts because we do not want to admit that we owe so much of what we are to the efforts of someone else.

SHE SAT AT the next table, so pleasant-looking, so beautiful, her mouth so red and perfectly formed, her teeth so superbly white, her eyebrows arched so nicely above her elegantly soft brown eyes that I wanted to go to her and touch her and mumble whatever words I could find to say.

And then, after a moment, she spoke: "Those goddamned Kennedys: they're just going to let the niggers take over the country."

A MAN WITH a purpose does not think, is not free enough to think. He is too committed. It is the purposeless man, the man with a little time on his hands, who becomes curious, wonders, speculates. It is simply a case of being *available* for thinking — of the mind, out of its idleness, suddenly saying Hmmm, have you thought of this?

FOR A LONG TIME I went into bars — to have a beer, yes, but mainly to overhear talk, to see if the common man might have a truth I was failing to get from books. I was hoping that one day I would be sitting in a darkened lounge and would hear The Great Stunning Insight fall from the lips of a construction worker or life insurance salesman.

But, of course, I never did. The years passed and the same Budweiser clock kept glowing on the wall; the same after-work sadnesses were exchanged among the same dreary loners at the bar.

. . . There was a truth available in the gloom, sure enough, but not the kind I wanted.

YOU MUST PERIODICALLY stick holes in the thin veneer of Now in order to let the past breathe easily underneath.

MY MIND IS LIKE a wound; experience irritates it, keeps it bleeding its words.

REELING, DELIGHTED, with the discovery of Knut Hamsun. . . .

For the first time since Dostoyevski such a sense of rooms and streets and weathers and excitable men and excitable women. Men with mud on their boots, men in tattered coats or with broken backs, feverish men who suddenly stop pacing the city streets and stride violently out into the country.

Extravagance, whimsy, exclamation marks, surging monologues. And *doctors as men* — Chekhov doctors.

ART RESULTS when the passion of living becomes too much to bear. If there is no passion, or if it can be tolerated, there is no art.

I BREATHE EASIEST when I am fully on the land. I look out to the day unnervously. I am friends with air, with grass, with country sounds. The heat of the sun delights me, and the cool of shady places. . . . I listen and touch and see and life seems very real.

All acts seem right in the country: a tractor plowing in a field; a gate closing; a woman hanging washing on a line; a window facing toward the afternoon; ants crawling.

There is time for sitting down and time for walking about; there is no need for hurry. I move to the tempo of dogs barking, flowers growing, cows eating in a pasture.

SOMETIMES IT SEEMS that I just can't stand the weight of so much long living.

THE SUN, the blinded eye of God, revolving endlessly in the sky. . . .

Once sighted, once knowledgeable, once cognizant of all things beneath its gaze.

Now seared over by the terrible blaze of its own unrelieved creativity, by its own first wild fierceness. Now, a mere formality in the universe, a vestige left over from more convulsive, more primitive days.

I'M TIRED of people who can't give-and-take. I'm tired of easing around temperaments like a Japanese house-boy in soft slippers. I'm tired of egos and their luxuriating foliage which must never be touched harshly else the petals collapse inwardly in a fiercely protective heap.

IT IS OF no greater value to know truths than to remain ignorant of them. In this world, nothing helps.

MAYBE YOU KNOW the feeling when a dentist has at last finished drilling out the cavity of a decayed back tooth and begins to pack the filling into the hole. Over and over you feel him pressing and cramming the soft metal in place; over and over you feel the forceful but gentle and somehow rather pleasant crunching.

That's what I think of when I think about good writing: that space between the lines of print being crunched full of the soft metal of delight and love which the writer feels for the things he writes about. When that space is properly filled — utterly, every molecule — then the words are fixed and solid on the page, bound by the metal-firm strength of the writer's passion and concern.

SOMETIMES MY WIFE watches my roamings about the

house — the standing at a window, the looking out for a while, the walking back through the rooms; the sitting in a chair, the staring out of it, the rising, the starting to walk again.

My wife feels toward me as she would toward a family dog or cat who might keep pacing about or scratching at the bottom of a door: "If he could only tell me what's wrong so I could help him. If only he could talk. Maybe he's hungry — though surely not; not after that dinner he ate. Or thirsty . . . or cold. Maybe it's worms. I wonder if he needs some sort of good pill."

I listen to her thinking about me and I, too, wish that I suffered from an empty belly or case of worms. I wish I were in need of such a simple, direct remedy.

THE TRUTH that we can never adjust to: That the dimensions of life are unknown, that there are no limits, no certainty. Once the child leaves the security of home, there is never any security for him again until he finds a genuine home of his own.

SPENDING PART of my life walking up the steps of a high tower — then reaching the top and discovering that Camus had already walked up the other side.

THE JUAREZ MOUNTAIN stretches behind itself, unseen, into farther distant mountains and farther distant space. Daily it sits, sphinx-like, in its own deep shadow, in its Mexican saucer-land, quietly watching the parade of fellow mountains going northward across the Rio Grande.

During the hot midday hours it maintains itself in a private, inviolate calm: a dark-sheened puma stretched within a shadowed cage of desert air. And as evening comes, as the air softens and the heat leaves the land, it fades into an even deeper puma-mood — its catamount power unsprung, ready for other desert days.

DAILY LIVING: dropping a nickel into a deep wishing well and never hearing it hit bottom.

(Life, to be lived with lesser pain, must be a continuous giving, with no thought of returns. It is the preoccupation with returns, with rewards for the job done or intended, that causes the fretting. It is almost too hard a lesson to learn — to accept the fact that the wishing well has no bottom. Yet happiness will never come as long as you wait there at the well's edge, listening for echos.)

A WRITTEN LINE, to me, must be like a suspension bridge stretched above space very gracefully, resting only at its either end. (Is it lyricism I always want, minus the nightingales and tender boughs?)

THROUGHOUT THE CONVERSATION the fair-skinned Mexican bar owner sat with his head cocked to one side, listening, weighing. Occasionally he leaned over on the cafe table and twisted and retwisted the ends of his light-brown moustache. He kept his red, moist lips in an amused pout.

The two transients at the table, one Negro, one white, had been drinking their beer slowly. Both had on dirty, wrinkled clothes. The broad-shouldered Negro wore a gray golf cap and a black jersey with a rip down the side. He spoke quietly and used perfect grammar. The white man, in his early 40's, seemed to be a hobo and part-time laborer, yet when he spoke his words were well formed, his voice resonant, his attitude calm and knowing. He was like a handsome Jim Casy out of *The Grapes of Wrath*.

What amused the bar owner was the story the white man was casually telling: that he had stood beside a track in Deming, New Mexico, earlier that afternoon and, through will power, had brought the 3:35 Southern Pacific passenger train to a halt. Three times during the previous week he had done that, he said, in three different Arizona towns.

The Negro looked ahead into the magazine rack and sipped at his beer; the white man talked slowly, confidently; the Mexican bar owner twisted his moustache, deeply amused.

ANOTHER IN A SERIES *of Will Nots, Can Nots, and What Nots; This One Being, On the Business of Having to Pick Out*

Names and Assign Them to People in Stories so as Not to Use the Original Name of the Person You had in Mind: That is, Knowing Mr. Apple and Calling him Mr. Crab.

Oh, indeed: reach into your basket of tricks and find appropriate names for the people you are writing about. Call them Ishmael if you want but by all means select a bunch of names and tie them like laundry tags to your characters. This is called peopling your fictional world. Solemnly create this roster at random; call your hero Paul or Irving or Roscoe.

. . . Yes, you do it, but not me. I don't know any of these people and do not care to. My mind and body do not know Donald Steele or Marsha Hunt or Old Man Wyandott; why should I take these disembodied names and sheath the people I *do* know, I *do* care about, and then set about trying to make them real for others. They would be unwelcomed guests inside me. They would stand awkwardly in my mind like stick figures on an artificially lit and deserted stage, painfully obedient to my prompting cues, trying to mouth some "bright" or "interesting" speech for the edification of Literature.

What a parade of dummies I would sweat into action from my brain and try to keep moving from page to page. What an artless chain gang they would be, having no more signficance than a collection of small Buddhist temple bells tinkling in an idle wind — and entirely lacking their charm. And what a relief it would be for reader and author alike when it was all over, when these painted mannequins breathed their last: when they would gratefully die and remain buried within their pages, hardened into bitter tombs of print.

No, whatever I may be, I am no novelist, with characters to be artificially named and manipulated.

WHAT COULD MEANING *be*, for God's sake, if human experiences are meaningless?

I LIKE TO SEE Mexican women waiting at residential bus

stops in the late afternoon, enjoying, in solitude, their after-work cigarette.

I SIT BESIDE the Rio Grande in the Upper Valley, watching it move through the call of mourning doves and the shedding of cottonwoods. White fluff soars out of trees and drifts easily in the breeze before coming to the water in graceful fusings. The morning is overcast, and when the sun finally breaks through the clouds it is pleasant to look across the river and see the sand hills stark and bright in the west.

Salt cedars stand in their gray-green clumps, there is a cool ten o'clock breeze, doves call from unseen places. . . . Even though the Rio Grande is only a reminder of the river it used to be, it is a proper river nevertheless: it still carries, for the desert-living person, the lure of water within its banks. Nature still lives in the casual blurps and gurgles that rise out of its depths, in the slow passing of leaves and sticks, in the bright sheen of the water as it spreads in a sweep of wind.

LIFE: a temporary displacement from the eternal constancy of Oblivion or God or Whatever. Having life: being temporarily lodged in a crack between Oblivions.

I SIT AMONG Mexicans after dark at the downtown plaza, calmed by their poverty, their humanness.

Women rest babies in their laps; men look out from benches. There is always a little quiet talk going on.

They know exactly who they are: they are mothers and workers and old people and men. And they know what they are doing; they are waiting on buses, or merely sitting, or just in the midst of the slow passing of another night.

I wait there with them in the plaza, in the warm darkness, grateful to be sharing the quiet companionship of their lives.

PEEL THE HIDE off a man doing things *competently* and

you will find a man sick at heart. For it has ever been so: that doing a job merely well is a kind of slow-motion death. It is only when a fresh wind comes upon a man's blind side and catches his competency off guard — suddenly touches the skin hidden beneath the accreted shell of skills, poses, wearisome routines — that he stands the slightest chance of rejoining life: of knowing once again, as he did in childhood, the miracle of doing something because he likes it, of doing something out of joy.

THIS I KNOW FOR SURE: that if I had ever listened to any of the people who, at one time or another, were willing to give me their advice about writing, I would have never ended up publishing a damn thing.

BUS STATION PEOPLE: The young woman sits on her waiting room bench, a shapeless mother trying to manage three kids while her fat husband, in his blue fishing cap, chews on his toothpick and enjoys himself with a new-found friend across the aisle.

She sits in her faded blue dress, her underarms sweating, one fat leg and knee methodically bouncing the baby. Vericose veins have begun to make purple lumps in her legs. She wears a constant frown.

The husband laughs loudly as he talks to a slickhaired young man who has a bottle of tequila in a shopping bag. The husband lolls his toothpick in his mouth and snaps his fingers at the jokes the slick-haired fellow is telling. Every now and then he notices his five-year-old making a pest of himself with the other passengers — and his wife pulling the boy back from the middle of the aisle — but he keeps on talking. Taking care of the kids isn't a man's work where he comes from. . . .

The woman continues to look out gloomily as she trots the baby, jerks at the arms of the boy, scolds the yellow-haired daughter who leans against her and whines. Yet every once in a while it happens: Whenever the husband snaps his fingers and takes off his fisherman's cap and begins to fan himself — in appreciation of his companion's bedroom tales — the woman lets an indulgent half-smile come to her lips. For she simply cannot help herself: The lazy good-for-nothing across the aisle is her husband and, to her, something special. She knows, of course, that the circumstances of their lives will always stay the same: that he will play Big-Time Charlie with each new pal — sitting with his legs wide apart, his pants hitched up on his white, fat, freckled legs — and she will be there in the background, yanking at the kids, cuffing them, trotting each new baby on her knee. But she knows something else too: that into the unrelieved drabness of her old life *he* had come — had joined himself to her — and that was enough of an act of salvation to keep her smiling her thin, wan, begrudging smile as she watches him hold court. For she knows that in the soured-laundry smell of life he can enjoy himself, and she cannot — lacks the talent, somehow, for feeling pleasure — and that makes all the difference.

WHAT I AM DOING in my brief sketches is not *describing* a thing — a door slamming, a bird sitting, a mountain lying across the earth. Rather, I am trying to transfer that thing — intact, still breathing, still possessed of beauty or mystery — from its old habitat to new surroundings. And if such a thing had any original significance then I would like to let it have it on my page. I don't want to take pictures — to merely paint things with accurate and careful words. I don't want just to preserve life. I want to raise it to still another power. I want to give it, if I can, its immortality.

ERAS PASS, and whole blocks of cities are left to winos, thugs, indigents, and poets.

IT IS TWELVE O'CLOCK at night and I must put the sick cat in the garage. With her purring contentedly against my side I step out into the cool October air. Fellini, the big pet lamb — the long-tailed, badly spoiled child — immediately comes across the back yard in his sauntering yet quick-footed gait. He knows it is improbable that I am going to feed him again but then there is always a chance. He sniffs at my legs and shoes as I open the side door of the garage and put the cat inside. The cat likes it there, and so does Fellini. That is where his feed is kept. He sticks his nose through the partly opened door. "Get back, Fellini," I say, and he retreats a pace. I close the door and then hunker down to pass a few midnight words with him. I ask him how things are going, if life is treating him well, and he sticks his head close to my leg and breathes contentedly against it. After a bit I rise and move on to the small ligustrum tree by the back door where Mrs. Garvin, the bantam hen, is roosting. As I address her and smooth a couple of fingers along her back, she responds with little singing, sighing croons from her throat. I bid her goodnight, go inside the house, and lock the door. Through the kitchen window I see Fellini lingering near the steps, looking in wistfully. Finally he decides that I will not be coming out any more for a while and begins to move along, head down, back into the darkness of the yard.

CURIOUS: why do fat men always seem to wear white cotton socks?

EVERYONE IS A CRIPPLE (I was 32 years old before I learned *that* little truth).

IT IS IN HEARING old songs again and feeling the goosebumps rise throughout your body that you suddenly realize how much, for you, *the past was never completed.* A hundred familiar doors are still ajar inside you, and to hear the songs is to look again down yawning passageways of the past, to feel once more the cold drafts coming off broken dreams and love affairs.

It is always with a sense of unfinished business, then, that you write, trying to do at last what you could never do before: give to things a final shape that pleases you.

Sometimes, with luck, you actually can: by calling forth imagination, and using the special power over past events that time alone ultimately gives a person, you can say the magic words that will cause one of the doors to swing shut on its painful memory. At other times, however, despite the same careful attempt at mastery, the words fail and the door remains open as though rusted into place by permanent tears — as if allowing its room of old defeats to go on echoing for a lifetime its nostalgic melodies.

SOME PEOPLE KNOW statesmen, movie stars, entrepreneurs; I know chickens, cats, and a broken-legged rabbit.

DEATH — THE THOUGHT, the fact, the *inevitability* of it — has shaped my life since age five. I cannot conceive of how my life would have progressed had I been without the knowledge and fear of death.

COLLEGE BOY, 1963: It is Saturday afternoon and a young man is sweeping out his second-hand car. He wears a worn bathing suit, sneakers, a flowered sport shirt. Watch him, for he may be dangerous. . . . Perhaps I had better explain.

The young man owns very little besides the car and his bathing suit — some extra clothes, several cardboard boxes full of books, a typewriter. Everything that he possesses, however, will fit into his car. Such mobility is part of the reason why he is dangerous — to himself, to the status quo, to his well-to-do neighbors in the block.

. . . Since he is young he is very much the critic and faultfinder. He is good at smelling out hypocrisy and has little or no truck with compromise. Also he is not at all concerned with the fact that people will go on living after his death just as they were living before his birth. He does not dwell on such a continuity because he is too involved in his own life, in the life of the present.

At twenty he knows things. He knows about love-making on quilts, and beer, and Raymon Magsaysay, and the old movies of

W. C. Fields, and dicotyledonous plants, and the oil depletion allowance, and Fyodor Dostoyevski. He knows these things and more, for he is a college boy.

He knows quite a few things, really, and thus as he sweeps the dust from the floorboards he feels strong and capable and ready — he, this innocuous-looking young fellow with the white hairy legs, the worn bathing suit, the two-tone second-hand car.

And it is because of this knowledge — and because of the even greater innocence that lies beneath it like the white fruit of an apple within its glossy red rind — he is dangerous. For he is going to act one day soon. He may protest a law or throw a brick or march with a crowd — all depending on what it is that he believes he knows — but whatever he chooses to do it will leave its mark on the man that is growing within him. And no matter whether it is a brave act, or a cowardly act done as the member of a mob, or merely a senseless, futile act better left undone, it will cost him something that he will remember to his dying day. For with that act he will lose his youth.

JOHN UPDIKE: he has, greatly, the capacity for the right observation. But so much that he does is over-reaction, exaggeration. Everything he touches luxuriates. Simple things, that should rightfully remain simple things — they are forced to burst into flower under his pen. A rock is not allowed to be a rock; it is forced to be Itself Unbound, a thing dancing and exploding before your eyes — a rock of frenzied atoms, a Rock as Author's Conception and Idea. Through his high artistry he manages to rob things of their essential peace and being. His is a hand that constantly reaches into the cavity of a man and brings out not bone and flesh and blood but, instead, jewels and Roman candles and many-angled mirrors

(is it that I come from a place of great space and constancy; a place of long mesas and deep sun; a place of long-sitting Mexicans? is it that I come from a place that always manages to say:

wait, pause a minute; let me show you a glimpse of how eternity is?

(is it that I still want a writing that allows a geometry in life — that allows elemental surfaces and lines to retain their dignity, their force? am I uncomfortable in an ever-exploding world of relativity: still a Steinbeck and not a Joyce?).

THAT HANDWOBBLING and elbow-jiggling grace of certain lithe Negroes — as though their extremities have been afflicted somehow and need to be gently cushioned on the air as they walk.

I DO NOT WISH to do any of the things that people do to earn money in this society.

POSSIBLY THE ONLY magazine I have not submitted a manuscript to is *The Cleft Palate Journal.* I am not sure how much longer I can hold out.

L., THE CONTINUALLY unmarried young woman, the continual holder of some address like Apartment #33, Wilshire Terrace; one whom you always associate with a row of mail-boxes in a silent hallway, with the small name card identifying her — verifying her existence in the world (: a name on a mailbox in Houston, Texas, her lone badge and credential); L., the efficient working girl, someone's steady Girl Friday.

HAUNTED BY THE sound of names: Martha Navarro . . . Gary White . . . Velia Sambrano . . . Tom Price. Haunted by the sound of my own name, too, mixed in with the others: "So long, Mr. Bode. . . . See you tomorrow, Mr. Bode. . . . Goodbye, Mr. Bode."

Hundreds of names — all of them once meaningful, all of them once joined in the common classroom cause.

What is it worth — all those intense days, those daily meetings and sharings? Were those names really so important that you should have bothered putting down opposite them, in the grade-book, so many marks? Was any of that business consequential: those months and years of teaching? Which was more real, the classful of faces at three o'clock or the empty room at three forty-five (with just the ghosts remaining: the aisle-jutting desks, the scattered papers on the floor, the silence)?

ON THE BERLIN stories of Christopher Isherwood:

He is the only writer I can think of right now who writes of homosexuals with a sense of balance, a light sure touch, and humor. When Isherwood's homosexual — or bi-sexual or non-sexual, whoever the man may be — comes onto the page, he comes first of all as a *person,* with his sexuality only a part of him: it is never a whirling, tormenting cloud, obscuring his personality. Isherwood writes with an old-Greek air of calmness that is missing from the works, say, of James Baldwin or William Goyen. The scenes which appear before the reader are so well filtered through the author's serene temperament that there is none of the guilt-ridden, furrowed-brow tenseness that authors usually show when describing a world inhabited by multi-sexuals. There is no lush foliage here, no stylized anguishing. Indeed, Isherwood's Berlin is like a Gothic seashore where people show themselves to be either amusing or weak or grotesque yet nevertheless themselves — real and recognizable.

Isherwood uses — rather than *displays* — a great talent in pre-senting the moods and people of Berlin in the early '30s. This talent is deceptive since the writing is so casual, the art so artless. Isherwood has the knack — as Mark Twain had, and Colette — of saying a perfectly ordinary thing so well that it becomes extraordinary perfect. Yet he never strains after effects, never tries for word flashiness. (The trouble with nearly all the celebrated young writers of today is that they are too damn word-conscious, too bent on stunning the reader. The Updikes and their kin do not seem to understand that life is not dazzling us moment after moment; that air and water and earth and wood are not made up of bits of jewelry; that the world is not an enlargement of the human nervous system). With Isherwood one feels comfortable, knowing that he speaks with a good voice that will tell you about interesting and compelling people and events — and tell about them well — yet will never adopt poses just to show you that he is, indeed, an Artist at Work.

Isherwood has the right flair for moving himself deftly among the people he knows and among the days he has lived in: he is right for Berlin, and his excellent stories present us not only with one corner of the world in the 1930's but with something else even more unique: that rare event which occurs when place, in joining personality, forms a reality that seems like truth.

DEATH, PAIN, and despair are like patient pendulums that swing across human life in monstruous silent arcs. Whenever they happen to pass near us — and miss — we compliment ourselves for being invulnerable. Convinced that the forces of darkness have forever fled the light, we continue to putter about smugly in the little gardens of our delusion — never seeing the shadow that is sweeping in close to clip us from behind.

IF I COULD paint pictures, I would paint this one, of a filling station in spring:

The sun is shining; it is a warm, slow-paced April afternoon.

A man is standing in one of the doorways of the station, drinking a coke, looking out. He is backed off for a moment from the day.

In another stall a Negro worker in rubber boots washes a car. He moves about routinely, soaping, rubbing, spraying. Music comes from a small portable radio sitting nearby on a ledge.

Over the doorways of the stalls the green Texaco letters look neat and responsible in the afternoon light: MARFAX LUBRI-CATION WASHING AUTOMOTIVE SERVICE.

There are no cars right now at the gasoline pumps; the station floor is a quiet, smooth stretch of three o'clock concrete, partly in shadow.

A man comes around the corner of the station from the rest room. He has the air of subdued personal satisfaction — the mild, mid-afternoon optimism which says I-have-taken-time-out-for-a-good-leak-and-now-I-am-ready-to-go-again-for-a-while. The man goes over to a stall filled with rows of green and golden cans of oil. He begins whistling as he selects a fan belt from the white-painted back wall. With his foot he slides a tire tool out of the way; it begins to shine in the doorway light as a surge of traffic goes by in the street.

LIFE MAKES GOD APPEAR to be a kind of psychopath: His putting into man the very characteristics which doom him to pain and despair and unfulfillment.

THE SNOTTINESS of those who do the same small job effi-ciently for years.

YOU SEE A BUTTERFLY jitterbugging its way among the flowers, across a green yard—like youth, caught in the sun.

THIS INSANE, magnificent, meaningless, overwhelmingly important world.

I FIND THAT MY FACE offends a number of people I meet at school. It seems much too solemn for public display — incap-able, apparently, of registering anger or joy or any of the other easily identifiable teacher-emotions.

But why should my outside-of-class solemnity bother anyone, I have asked myself. If it so happens that the experiences of your life have led you to the point that it is often easier for you to contain your feelings than demonstrate them facially — as others often do — why should this be of concern to anyone?

It shouldn't be, unless you are hired by the public schools — which seem to require that a teacher always indicate whether he feels jolly or mean-tempered or pleasantly casual. Since I tend to control my feelings, letting them show as I choose, I am considered suspect by my fellow teachers. They look into my face and do not like what they see — or at least, they do not *know* what they see, which makes them uncomfortable, puzzled, and vaguely irritated.

Let me say this: during spare moments of the school day my mind is generally concerned with matters unacademic. I use whatever free time I have to reconsider something I have been reading or thinking and to put those reflections down on paper. Yet I always make a conscious — yea, *strenuous* — effort never to inflict the depths of my personal concerns upon the people around me. I bend over backwards to show the basic amenities and attempt in good faith to carry out all the duties charged to me. But in doing so I am still controlling myself, doing and saying things in a somewhat measured, careful way — and this, too, infuriates the other teachers. For it seems to point up the absence in me of "school emotions," a lack of preoccupation with what is supposed to be the teacher's daily burdens. I do not appear to be taking very seriously the world of my colleagues; I am not committed to their values and am obviously not playing their ball game (— I do not eat with them or smoke in their lounges or pass my off-moments in their presence). Thus they listen to whatever words I say and they look fleetingly at my face — and are made suspicious. I *seem* to be just another teacher, yes; but then again, they just can't be sure. . . .

THERE ARE EXTENDED moments during spring afternoons when the mixture of greenery and hidden bird sounds and shadows and sunlight, washed by casual movements of the wind and the drone of slow airplanes, open up emotional passageways so subtly profound that they seem to stretch completely through your mind and memory to a kind of primordial heaven. And if you add immaculate white stone houses with red tile roofs, and elm-lined courtyards with low brick walls, it becomes too much. You are translated into trees and air and sun-lit space and you cease to be you: you become the afternoon, the spring moment of timeless beauty and delight.

LET'S SAY YOU ARE nearly crazed, walking the streets in the afternoon, unable to write. You have exhausted all pursuits: you have walked, read, looked, sexed, thought, but to no avail. You are at the point of a physical and emotional eruption — of suddenly spurting blood out of the top of your head — when finally you walk into a dark, cool hotel lobby and sit in one of the overstuffed chairs and begin to put words down against a piece of paper. The effect is like having one who has deeply sinned to suddenly make peace with his God: having the Grace that exists at the core of all life to rescue you from the dead-end of reality and show you the smooth open road of imagination.

IT IS A WONDER that all human beings do not become insane as a matter of course.

THE WORLD AS IT exists is that perfect spike upon which minds can burst themselves like so many fragile balloons.

THERE HE IS, a beautiful, fastidious dachshund, sitting in front of my chair and looking up at me with his dark sad eyes. And as he sits, so quietly, in such a warm comfortable room, somewhere out in space there is that damn sun shooting its flame into the eternal night.
How can the human mind ever learn to gaze, on the one hand, at the familiar realities of the earth and, on the other, at the infinitude that surrounds it?

I was walking through a hot westside suburb, and it was as though El Paso had suddenly been paralyzed by an invisible nerve gas. The neighborhood was that deathly still. At eleven-thirty in the morning — ordinarily a time when plates are being set on dinner tables, refrigerator doors being opened and shut — there was no sound anywhere. I could not even hear a baby crying. The lawns streched out in neat and orthodox greenness, slender elms and cottonwoods stood placidly along trimmed sidewalks, cars sat on their cement driveways, but there was not a sign of life anywhere.

Yet I knew that people were inside their houses: the cars were there, a few water sprinklers were going, and sometimes as I passed a window I could see the square bluish light of a television set. Human life definitely existed there in the suburb; it had not vanished.

Walking along, I tried to identify the quality of the silence that filled the streets. It was not the vacant sadness of Sunday — that curious, empty time when it seems that all the bright leaves of life have turned brown at the edges. Nor was it the deep quietness of the country, or the unsettled stillness of a city at night. It was . . . yes, that was it, perhaps: like the desolate silence of the moon. It was an emptiness so stark and loud that it almost imitated sound. And as I passed on through the suburb it was as though the hot silent streets had finally become my own blood pumping through my ears: a violent noiseless pulse no longer outside my head but thundering within.

My lovely child, born of my blood and the world's mystery: she will never know how wildly I took her hand and kissed it in the middle of the night, in the dark of the quiet, sleeping house. That intensely warm two-year-old's hand — she will never know with what anguish I first soothed it; or how, gaining peace, I slowed into long contemplative strokes, calmed by its touch.

My child, asleep, so wholly oblivious of pain, of danger, of existence itself; not knowing how long I stood there above her, silent, curious, regarding the fragility of her small breathing form.

My child, so deeply dreaming with her groaning little sighs, so entirely at peace with this world I cannot understand (a world that someday —oh, yes, I can bet on it — will yawn and in its boredom break my child in two; in one mindless stroke bring ugliness and pain and give the lie to my moment of beauty in the dark).

THE GREAT BOOKS are within all of us; the letters of the typewriter keyboard are available to the many agile monkeys of our sensibilities. Yet — despair, despair — we do so very little in a lifetime. We can never get the monkeys' wandering hands to reach deep enough, often enough, into the jungle of our subconscious in order to begin their awesome tap-tap.

WELL-TO-DO WOMEN: In black Cadillacs and white gloves, their red-ringed Saturday morning smiles flashing behind cool, air-conditioned window panes, they sit securely as their sleek cars roll through gently curving streets lined with tall green trees and stately houses. Scrubbed and powdered and perfumed, their hands manicured and their legs sleekly sheathed within fine-mesh hose, they are El Paso's composed and elegant matrons. They taste the leisured life of Saturday morning like hummingbirds sipping bright red wine.

ONE CAN ONLY become what one *is*. No one could be Jesus except Jesus.

WHAT IS THE EFFECT of visiting old people when you are young: of being quiet in their presence, of seeing them with their wrinkled skin and unpleasant infirmities? (Do young people today visit old people much? Do they smell the closed-in rooms, the failing bodies? Do they stand in the gloom, the awesomeness, of great-grandmothers?)

IN OLD MESILLA: That lush tree-shaded back yard along the main canal in mid-afternoon. The pen of leghorn hens singing in the summer heat; the pen of elegant roosters with their sensual red combs. The many sparrows, high in pecan trees that are riverbank size, with great arcing branches. The sense of a nicely cluttered, old-person's place, with weeds, heat, red-and-black stains of fallen mulberries, deep summer fecundity. The grape arbor, huge virile sunflowers, peach trees taking the sun. The logs and tin cans half-buried in the undergrowth. The deep shadows on the tin roof of the unpainted barn.

THE DAILY NOTHING.

THE MORE I LIVE, the more it seems that the concept of sin was introduced by men in a desperate effort to preserve their sanity and their idea of God: for man seemingly has a great capacity for feeling his own guilt but could not long tolerate the idea that *God* is guilty.

I AM 33 and the facade of my personality remains smooth. But I cannot see how another ten years can pass without the great inner cracks finally showing through.

A BUTTERFLY in mid-morning, resting peacefully on dung.

I HAVE, CERTAINLY, a curious talent — warped, I suppose, by my delight in sensuously perceiving the physical world.
  To illustrate:
"It was a heat-filled July day, with clouds building from the east and great shadows on the mountains — a lazy day, with Mexican children playing outdoors in the shade, and dust, and white fluff drifting from the huge cottonwood trees along the canals. The sour smell of the Texaco refinery was in the air; small birds yelled from their hidden nests.
  "An old man sat on his small front porch, regarding the siz-

zling noon streets. It will rain again today, he thought."

. . . All right, there it is: nothing spectacular, of course, but a possible beginning for some story or other — a story I will never care to write. Why? What keeps me *sketching* — and ignoring stories?

Everyone else who writes wants to reveal the fabric of society, plot the happenings of a man's life, explore a mind or describe a character. But not me. Perhaps I want nothing more than to make words move gracefully, evocatively across a page. Perhaps, too, I feel that only the world that is closest to nature — the world of animals, children, old people, grass, sunlight, trees — lends itself best to such evocation: to a pursuit of beauty, to the poetic savoring of life. Perhaps to me the poetic savoring of life *is* life, *is* living, and to use words for any other reason than to glorify life is meaningless. And perhaps I feel that only through my kind of brief, casual sketches am I being true to the deepest urge within me.

I MARVEL THAT there are chemists and plumbers and mathematicians who spend their life's energy on compounds and wrenches and logarithms instead of simply standing around with their mouths open — agog over the mystery of the world's flesh and blood.

ALAS, POOR YORICK TEE, HEE! She was talking about an accident of the day before: a high school student had slammed his car into two young girls, killing them instantly. The girls had been walking home from school along a sidewalk when the car suddenly veered from the street and jumped the curb and slammed the two girls against a stone wall.

The woman was a small, gray-haired cafeteria worker who served teachers coffee every morning. As she talked she suddenly brightened: "Somebody said they was eating ice cream!" And she giggled. Her laughter wasn't loud and she did not even sound particularly frivolous. It was just that she was a little nervous and had let the giggle escape.

Her mouth kept the smile for a moment, grew uncertain, finally collapsed into seriousness. She turned away from the serving line and began placing doughnuts into the glass shelves.

I PUCKERED AND KISSED the air. It was to be sure a foolish smack, but not futile. It spoke for me, reaffirmed me to the world.

IF THERE IS, indeed, a God, and if indeed He made everything and everyone there is, has been, and ever will be: *What in the world does He want?* What can we do to repay Him — or make Him stop?

SOMETIMES THE SHEER GREENERY of my home country — arrived in after a long stay in the brown bare lands of West Texas — so shocks me, gives me such psychic goosebumps, that I would like nothing better than to go off in the woods somewhere and live as mindlessly as a toad.

IT WAS ONLY after I stopped trying to be everyone else on earth that I picked up the business of being myself again.

DARK HANDS REACHING into the cook's window of a cafe bearing clean stacked plates, a hot lunch, washed glasses. Negro hands glistening with dishwater, bearing this and that, disappearing, reappearing. Brown hands emancipated a hundred years ago, still reaching out into the white world from the kitchen.

I WOULD BE ROCKING ALONG, not feeling particularly down and out; then, without being fully aware of what I was doing, I would get into my car and start driving. I would just be vaguely dispirited or depressed, a little bit out of touch with the core of myself — as if I had been too long at someone's weekend party in too stiff a suit of clothes — and almost automatically I would head for the country, in a kind of blind faith that whatever was wrong with me could be remedied there.

THERE IS AS MUCH difference between the country and the city as between God and the church. The church, like the city, is always *one step removed* from essentials.

COMPETENT, FAST-MOVING repairmen who step around a broken washing machine or the bared motor of a car, whistling like psychotic canaries — moving briskly through the cascade of their own jittery, rhythmless noise.

AN HONEST WORD written down is an attempt on the part of the writer to give a name to something not yet specified in the world. It is doing what the Bible said that God once did in identifying the creatures of the earth — calling one *fish*, one *sheep*, one *man*. In his own determined way a person writing *is* the same as God; thus to write is an awesome act, not to be undertaken lightly.

Indeed, how often can one actually say to himself: I know this thing and I am ready to pronounce the sound of it: I have seen it in the morning and in the night, I have felt its essence move within me, and now I will put it forth to join other created things.

People are trying to say when they write: Here is the Truth created by me — and here is Me serving as truth. . . . It is what we do, and I think it is justified. For writing has always been the attempt to make one's own separate Bible, to immortalize, to walk on the water of life.

ZARAGOZA HIGHWAY on a winter's night: Walking along in the darkness, feeling that you are indeed at the mysterious edge of another country; knowing that this narrow highway, so dark and cold, spotted here and there by shadows of other lone walkers, is stretching out uninterruptedly across the whole solitary darkness of Mexico.

LIKE A SALMON working its way upstream, I keep fighting to remember that *it is all a gift: everything.* This self we drag around with us, this life we live: it is not ours.

WALKING UNDER TREES at night all men are mystics. (There are so few mystics in the world only because there are so few men out walking at night.)

WHAT A WRITER DOES is mark off a piece of land or group of people and stay right there working until he makes the land or the people his: the country becomes Faulkner Country, the people Steinbeck People. A man and his materials become so much one that they cannot be separated. And it's not just art; it's chemistry: hydrogen finds oxygen — marvelously, with beauty, for keeps.

Of course someone else can always try to take over ownership of that very same land or people or way of life, but it will probably not do him much good. He can never get a clear title. Someone may make another canoe trip down the Brazos River in November, say, but what he writes about it is apt to be pale stuff, or derivative. For John Graves has already made that particular trip, and felt it, and did the writing about it, and there is little way that further writing and feeling can bite more deeply into that same material.

This is what classic means: that the job was done, and need not be done again.

SOMETIMES THERE IS nothing more dismal looking than a regular-featured, well-fed, smiling, All-American Boy.

MUSIC ALONE can reach inside you and somehow manage to touch all the flowers that still grow among the debris of old emotions.

I WOULD LIKE to write paragraphs that kicked hell out of

a reader — that pulled the rug out from under his feet and put him back in the emotionally vulnerable, off-balanced position he was in before he began to think he had learned so damned much and began to forget about mystery and beauty and terror and awe.

I FIND IT a nice animal pleasure to take a cup of coffee over near the windows of the quiet school cafeteria and clean off a spot at a table and sit there for thirty minutes or so, drinking the coffee and writing a few self-satisfying words.

No teachers, no students at that nine o'clock hour. Only an un-hurrying Mexican janitor going by, a clump of keys jangling pleasantly at his belt, and in the long open kitchen Mexican women in white uniforms moving about among shining alumi-num pans.

The cafeteria is a good place to feel comfortable and private — where, gradually, little unobstrusive things seem to count. As you drink from the coffee cup and then slowly set it down, you watch the paper napkin absorb drops spilled in the saucer. The sight of brown creeping into white is definitely pleasing, and you want to smile. Considering this stained napkin for a moment, you think perhaps you might write a word or two about it — about why a napkin sitting under a coffee cup at nine in the morning is at least as glorious as a pope's skull cap.

Just sitting there in a state of well-being makes you remember similar states. As you look out the window past the sweep of school lawn you see a postman walking far off in the next block — sun on his helmet, letter pack shining — and he reminds you of a postman back in Kerrville, in earlier years. And then you re-member the story about Faulkner — the university postmaster — lounging in magnificent disdain among the growing piles of un-sorted and undelivered mail. But what you think about doesn't really matter: the point is that you are, indeed, thinking, your mind is solidly in gear. And you know that if you could keep on sitting there, taking a little coffee now and then and letting your mind do what it wanted to, your hand would soon be taking whatever pencil and paper was nearby and you would be writing. You would end up sitting there in that cool darkened cafeteria all morning long, letting the pencil fly in wondrous abandon.

But you cannot, of course. You are merely a public school teacher who has eased away from the crowd during your conference period. You are not an artist lounging in a Paris sidewalk cafe. . . . The bell will be ringing in a minute or two, and you still have to put your coffee cup in the dirty dish window as well as make the long hike back to your room — just as an interesting thought was coming, with its nice shape and what seemed to be its nice subtle overtones. . . .

SCENE: With his cap on, sitting in splotched white overalls and his leg propped against an open door, the lean housepainter sits in his car under a shade tree and munches his noon sandwich (— need I say that the weather is warm, and the car radio is on, and the lettuce is poking out between the bread?)

FACING LIFE MEANS facing death: another of those hard paradoxes.

I AM NOT VERY GOOD any more at being vibrantly human; I have faded some way. Thus on those days when a mood is lying across the land I can simply edge this thin remaining slice of me into unnoticed cracks in the air and become immensely still. I can watch and listen and sometimes actually perceive what is going on. It's as though the world short circuits for a moment through my senses, recording itself in a kind of emotional electrocardiogram.

I KNEW THE *alive* George Duderstadt — the shape of his head underneath a hat, his gait in the worn, runover boots as he walked across the back lots of the ranch. But I don't know the other one — the one out there in a Harper grave, the one barely two years old. Sometimes I wonder how long it will be before the two of them begin to cancel each other out — the live one and the dead — so that it will seem that neither of them ever existed at all, that both were part of some recurrent dream.

A WRITER KEEPS seeing a thing as he first saw it as a child. Thus as an adult he looks out at an afternoon and it has not changed: it is still as it first was when he had nothing else in the world to do except see and hear such a thing as an afternoon. To him, as to the child, an afternoon never becomes a means to an end — a time to sell shoes in, or drive trucks. It is not a vacant space to fill up but remains *an event in itself.* . . .

To a child living at four o'clock on a summer's day there are just two things that are real: himself and the afternoon; the perceiver and the perceived. That is why a writer who grows past childhood is always so sad about afternoons: the old attachment is supposed to be broken. An adult is not supposed to enjoy a time of day for itself — or merely exist in it, as one phenomenon within another. He is supposed to be out working and getting ahead (— especially getting ahead of things like *afternoons*). And yet, as the writer looks about him, there the afternoon is, as it always has been: the trees and shadowed grass and quiet buildings; the sound of hammers on distant roofs, and locusts, and sparrows; the steady heat and light.

But even if an afternoon does contain its own Garden of Eden, only those not fit for work are capable of enjoying it — and such people are doomed and cursed: the child, because he has to learn to outgrow afternoons, to become responsible, to become a productive, wage-earning citizen; and the writer, because he *cannot* outgrow them (and therefore can never keep from feeling guilty about not "working," about not doing what he doesn't want to do, about not pursuing dollars instead of beauty or truth).

Yet it is during an afternoon — one filled with heat and shade and stillness and the sense of the earth — that a person can most easily feel himself in love (— for even though other human beings are better to love than things of nature, they are much harder). There is no effort needed to love oats shining in a field or tree limbs moving in a breeze because one is not concerned with *himself* in this kind of love. He does not think of possible gain or loss, of future or past; he is concerned only with profound pleasures of being (and thus bears his own private witness to the fact that the pursuit of happiness is not a pursuit at all but a perceiving, a witnessing, an embracing).

THE SOMEWHAT ARROGANT fellow who carried his cup of coffee the entire length of the college snack bar with his fly open.

PARADISE   I was down at the bus station the other night, watching the people in the waiting room. They were hardly elegant. Travel-tired Negro women wrestled with their scab-nosed, crying babies; a young spastic threw himself forward on two wobbling canes. One toothless old woman with bursting-fat ankles inched along in faded house slippers while thin, unshaven men with bloodshot eyes stared out the glass doorway. A huge, dull-eyed Navajo in a straw hat wandered past looking forlorn; two West Coast teddy boys with beatle shoes and wrinkled, tight-legged pants argued and smoked and banged viciously at the pin ball machines. And old broken men sat on benches, slumped into their coats.

Yet as I watched them in all their waiting room grotesqueness — the halt and lame and put-upon and unredeemed — I had a curious vision of what Heaven must be like. I found myself staring into space, into Heaven, and the people I saw there walking slowly side by side were those same graceless travelers of the bus station. It was like seeing into the hold of a cosmic slave ship where manacled, starving, reeking prisoners were chained together in a swarming mass. Paradise, the vision seemed to say, was wherever human beings were kings — in all their ruined and unlovely mortality.

WHAT IS ONE DAY, one human being? They are everything, and they are nothing.

TWO CONTENTED HENS, singing as I watch them. Two
hens filled with table scraps and looking around for new worlds
to conquer. . . .
The January afternoon is cold but pleasant. The sun, keeping
up appearances, has managed to stay out, and early winter shadows
are beginning to streak the ground. Sparrows find the four o'clock
air to their liking and sweep down from neighboring trees to
scout eagerly about.
An airplane drones by. The two elms by the garage look gray
and bent.
. . . My back yard. My house. And as I stare out into the afternoon I feel like saying, "Yes, and my life, too — but what of it?
Those two speckled hens with their shreds of lettuce — they seem
to be doing all right, and that's fine, of course. But me — where
in the scheme of back yards and winter days is *my* lettuce, *my*
fulfillment?"
And I begin wondering if man has ever fitted anywhere — if
that is not his great sorrow: knowing that a shadow sliding
through a fence, birds flocking to the ground, somehow *belong*
to life; and that he, this strange lost figure out of the land of the
gods, can only stare in wonder at the ceaseless mystery of his surroundings.

GOD SAVE US from certain ambitious women who, in the
long run, never do the truly creative work but merely want to.

THREE LANK GUITAR PLAYERS at "The Green Frog," eyes
half closed, swaying from side to side like a trio of somnambulant
mothers rocking guitar-babies to sleep.

THE MAN WHO looks up at strangers as they pass his booth
in a cafe, the man who stares into other cars while he waits at a

traffic light: aren't they revealing a dissatisfaction with self and hoping that the face of a stranger will somehow provide them with a sudden clue?

Perhaps it can even be said that having curiosity about people and their situations is not genuine curiosity at all but rather a sign of continuous discontent. . . . Does a self-satisfied, truly integrated person have much curiosity? Isn't he interested only in the fulfillment of his own desires?

Haven't I been looking endlessly into the faces of others in the hope of discovering the lost face of Me?

PEOPLE HAVE ALWAYS written stories because they have wanted to tell of a hero, a grave happening, a great deed. In 50,000 B. C. you didn't sit around a campfire and listen to Armogot tell how Muloop picked his nose all the way from the cave to the boneyard and back. Armogot *celebrated* something for his listeners; he told of strength or achievement or mystery or, in his own way, beauty.

Since those days we have refined the subjects of our celebration, but our instincts — at least mine — still respond most strongly to those things which seem to reflect the inherent truth and mystery and beauty and *worthwhileness* of the world. The world is positive, not negative, our instincts tell us, and we are always drawn to those myths and tales and stories which tell of such a world — or tell of men trying to sustain or help create that world.

With God currently out of Heaven and nothing much available to take His place, it is somewhat unfashionable to speak of the *glories* of living. Glories are held suspect. But if I had to say right now what my creed of writing and living is, I would have to say, unfashionably, that it is to celebrate the glories, large and small, of the world I live in, despite the obvious and unceasing hell that goes along with it.

WE DID NOT have poverty in my home town when I was a boy. There were people who were poor, of course, but they were not called that. They were simply referred to by their last name, and since everybody knew what that name implied there was no need to say anything further.

Negroes and Mexican-Americans were not poor because they were not white. Only whites could be people enough to be poor. Except that there were no white people in town, either, because white people did not need to think of themselves as being white: they had the luxury to be just people. The rest were called niggers and meskins — and that too, in 1940, was all that needed to be said.

IT IS MEANINGLESS to say it, no one really believes it, there is nothing to do about it once it is said, but nevertheless it is true: We know nothing.

We work, and the years slide past, and the people around us live and die, and despite the many competencies we possess we still end up lacking all the fundamental answers to all the fundamental questions. We destroy — and learn too late the price we pay for our destruction; we produce — and find that what we produced is not really ours to keep. We exist for a while within the steel bubble of our ignorance and our illusions — feeling superior to the baboon and the snail — only to discover that we too belong to history and to nature.

We do many significant things and assume that by doing them we are learning what we need to know. We confuse energy with understanding, and then grow old — amazed at our emptiness.

THE *mystique* of the Other Sex — that strange and constant awareness of femaleness which makes a man willing to serve — so to speak — another master. A woman's foot, half-raised, slipping into sheathing nylon hose; the sudden faint aroma of face powder; the white skin of belly and thigh suggesting an inner body richness. . . .

I SUPPOSE JUNG is the thinker I go to with the greatest respect — and follow, in his easier writings, with the greatest intensity. He seems closest to being the Universal Man, plunging into the depths of this dark business of living and yet always managing to emerge again — if not serene at least unshattered.

ROMANCE IS MUSIC, the smell of bermuda grass, a girl, all the vague yearnings of youth. Romance is when you have not learned how to defend yourself.

I HAD RATHER read Steinbeck at his best than any other writer except Faulkner — for beauty, for serenity, for inner excitement, for companionship, for affirmation of my own vision and feelings. His language never falters. The words are not words of print on a page but images of stone that stretch like deep columns backward into time.

Steinbeck is a drawing together, a summing up of the *all* that one feels in life and a pinpointing of the effect of that all through the beautiful rightness of his words and feelings.

He reflects life and light. Faulkner is a plunging in, mostly, an uncompromising commitment to the depths of things.

A CHILD SITS PLAYING in the April sunlight; a soldier lies with his guts blown out in a ditch. . . .

I have always lacked a stance, one that would permit me to stand confidently astride the awful extremities of life.

OLD SITTING ROOMS where lone women relatives live among the smells of cooked cabbage and hairnets and soiled divans.

WHY IS IT that persons with good minds must always act so damn *prideful*, as if they had created themselves in their own image? They never escape from the grip of their intelligence — never are free enough to acknowledge the world outside them.

A MEMORY: One winter night when rain and cold should have been blanketing the land I took a walk through a small hill country town — and it was as though April had somehow been misplaced in December. The town was full of a balmy air coming with impossible gentleness out of the south — as if blowing mile after mile across moist hay fields and tall roadside grass. Sweet-smelling, content, it was a wind from my childhood — the wind that on spring evenings had swept across the freshly mowed lawns of churches and across parks full of great-trunked trees. It was the Wolfe-breeze of eternal youth and Old Catawba, of slim girls with tumbling hair, of nights full of the mystery of the earth. . . .

As I walked the dark streets of town the wind seemed like a lost innocence bathing my body again, trying to reclaim me for life. It condemned me — made me feel wasted, lost, futile, out of touch with the peace of myself and the quiet trees — and yet it was a promise too. The deeper I moved into the simplicity of the town and my past the more the wind became a brisk gesture on the part of nature to heal me: a cleansing force not only able to find its way beneath the false shell of my life but able to lay itself soothingly around my hidden, wasting core.

IT IS EASIER to be kind to dumb animals than to smart ones.

WHAT I AM can only be found in my childhood. That is the wood of my life; everything else is simply paint.

IT WAS FOUR O'CLOCK on an ordinary spring afternoon and Deborah was sitting in a grownup's chair, her legs dangling, her hands comfortably idle in her lap. She was watching me spin a top. And since she had nothing to accomplish, nothing to feel responsible for, nothing to decide, it was perfectly all right for her to sit there and be happy.

I looked across at her and knew why childhood is good, why children have joy in living: they simply have nothing they ought to do, no contribution to make out of themselves, no need to shape events. They can just *be* — for hours on end. They can sit in a chair, or chase a cat, or watch a strip of white sunlight playing against a window curtain. They let the world drift by like a huge lazy river and they sit along its banks, amused.

ONLY ANIMALS SEEM to make me comfortable — make me smile.

LANGUAGE is like a tireless jaunty walker through my head.

THE MANY MEN who spend their time hoo-rawing one another: the barbers and Lions Clubbers who begin with easy taunts and loud laughs, then move to the Great Laying On Of Hands, finally drop into the graver tones of Serious Business.

I SHOULD HAVE DONE *more*. It haunts me. . . . And yet it seems that I have always been ready to seize those moments in which I felt I had something to say.

Well, the fact is plain: I just didn't have much to say.

I WALK PAST HOUSES and yards of the entrenched and well-fixed, and there are features about them that immensely please me. Despite the fact that the people within the houses are perhaps not admirable human beings, the beauty of the grass, the trees, the shadowed porches still remains.

Yet I feel guilty for enjoying as I do the honeysuckle and roses of the merely prosperous — people with nothing going for them except a bank account — even though I realize that the honey-suckle is not to blame, if there is to be any talk of blame. The honeysuckle is simply deliciously fragrant — as much there in the rich man's yard as in the beggar's camp ground. It is an esthetic-ally good thing that is no less desirable just because a man sells Chevrolets or pushes dope in order to get enough money to buy it.

Let's put it this way: In the city only the prosperous have the wherewithal to duplicate some of the natural joys of the country.

They pour their dollars into gardeners and architects — thus creating expensively for themselves what the country does inexpensively for everyone.

My guilt comes from knowing what natural beauty is, loving it — and then, in the city, finding it mainly in the carefully nurtured parks and elegantly constructed houses of the well-to-do.

MEN IN THEIR 30s and 40s, with their new hostilities. They are getting pudgy in the middle, they drink to excess, they have become a little too dissatisfied with their jobs and wives. So — their bodies sagging, their lives increasingly humdrum — they look around irritably for someone to blame.

PRESERVE THE HERITAGE; preserve what was good. Reach back; find a way to keep the best. . . . Too many days pass, and gradually the things that once stood as little pinnacles of glory above the flatlands crumble and are buried. Before long we do not even remember what was worthy of saving.

This is the ache: a sense of responsibility for what was important, what was greater than you; a feeling that good things must be preserved: a feeling that although we don't know where we are going, we must know where we have been.

PEOPLE'S SHOES, so damn *human*-looking, all pointing to the aisle of the streetcar; such patient objects — unmoving, dusty, inelegant; graceless coverings for the walking machinery that is temporarily stilled.

LYING HAS ENABLED me to function in the world. I do not know what would have become of me if I had adopted a course of truthfulness with others. Probably I would have cracked up very early.

TELL IT, TELL IT: pour out that highly individualized business of *being you* in a particular time and place. If you do it well enough, maybe everyone will recognize himself in you.

AFTER HAVING A good writer tell you about Place Z, it is a disappointment to go there yourself. For if the writer really did his job he focused and clarified and selected bits and pieces so well that Place Z in reality can only suffer by comparison. It has too much to offer, it overwhelms you with detail.

A writer, then, always recreates places not only according to his knowledge of them but also according to his own point of view — that is, his temperament. They are not the towns or country-sides we see when we go there, for the ones before our own eyes appear surprisingly ordinary — lacking the grace or beauty or depth we found in the author's pages. If it is these we want then we must, rather humbly perhaps, open his books and visit on his terms alone, through his eyes.

HER MIND WAS a single straight wire of petulance, sending all her small, graceless thoughts humming up it like J. C. Penny money tubes.

WHY MUST CHILDREN first know joy—equate joy with life — and then learn afterwards they are supposed to do without it?

Why — in order to grow up — must you surrender joy? Why must life to the adult mean a grim juggling of money, duties, success, failure — but never joy?

Life turned gray for me when I was seventeen — when I went off to college and the Great World. I have been fighting ever since to regain that *something* I knew while growing up: that almost-happiness that came from being simply and supremely me.

Does the gaining of more *facts* about the nature of reality — about the world — have to bring unhappiness? Does awareness mean, necessarily, a fading of joy? Does the work that people accept for themselves when they grow up have to be, almost by definition, joyless: a *job*?

WRITING must come out of a quietness growing inside you.

A MEXICAN MAN met another Mexican man in a bar and

they couldn't stop smiling. They laughed, moved their hands in the air, touched one another on the shoulder, but still the joy of their meeting would not subside. They could not get enough of the sight of one another — could not get over the idea that each still walked the earth in his own pleasing uniqueness.

UNDERNEATH MY BLAND exterior I am anarchic.

BY LACKING REASONABLENESS, by being aggressively childish, anyone can seem powerful.

A PRIM-MOUTHED, spinsterish woman with glasses held about her neck on a chain, the train station cashier came out from behind the counter to arrange goods on a display case. She stood with her back to the magazine rack behind her, as if purposefully ignoring the bulging breasts and voluptuous lips of the cover girls on *Frolic* and *Sir* and *Escapade*. She carefully heaped up small pyramids of fruit, restacked candy bars, straightened boxes of Cracker Jacks; then, after taking the glasses from her narrow breast and placing them on her nose, she walked briskly back to her protective counter — with the cover girls on the magazine rack seeming to laugh and bulge and pant even more tantalizingly in her wake.

DO NOT FORGET *emotionality*, emotional force. Turn away from the dry mouthing of *words*. Plunge in, go beneath, or forget about writing.

THE SAP OF a cottonwood dripped down on my shirt, my hand — and I didn't mind. I was standing under it, loving the land, and that was all that mattered.

Yes, that's what I said: loving the land. That mourning dove off beyond the cotton field, giving its crooning song. And the mountains low in the distance, their sides solid angles of shadow and sun — as if made of hammered metal. A cow lowing. The leaves of the cottonwood above me moving in a cooling wind.

. . . Loving the land, and perhaps even loving myself because I had found, once again, such monumental peace.

I WALK AROUND and the people in the street — their shoes, elbows, gold fillings, varicose veins, breasts, hat bands — they are like extensions of my own body.

Yes, the Human Family — that's it. We are undoubtedly *one*.

I SUPPOSE THE CLOSEST I can come to describing what I feel when I am possessed by a need to write is this: It is like standing with your camera before a man, ready to take his picture. You focus on him, but as you focus you know that your camera is slowly turning into a magnifying glass — so that the skin of the man is no longer the skin seen by the naked eye but, instead, enlarged hairs and pores and bumps seen under magnification. But the microscope is gradually turning into a flourescope machine, so that you are next looking into the body of the man — the heart and liver and lungs beneath the skin. And the fluoroscope machine then changes into a microscope, immensely powerful, so that you are finally looking at the blood and cells and atoms and space of the man. Yet all this time the man is simply standing there, grinning toward the camera, being, apparently, just a familiar figure of a human being, and you just being the familiar figure of an ordinary photographer.

. . . That's at the root of my writing urge: to deal with a curious flowing out — almost like a tangible wave of protoplasm — from me to the thing I see. I can almost feel myself — my body, my imagination — becoming linked to the object beyond me in such a way that, for a moment, I receive the pulse of its life essence.

It amounts, somehow, to a kind of double-vision, double-feeling — of being a Siamese twin to the Otherness in life; an I-Thou, Martin Buber situation. It would explain, perhaps, the static quality in my reaction to things, a freezing of forward motion until the intensity of the experience-transfusion has taken place: a pausing, always, to take brief snapshots of life but hoping with each photograph to penetrate, say, through the bark of a tree into its pith: into the cells, essence, spirit, and whatever else that, God-like, lies hidden at the core.

DEBORAH, HER SMALL delightful head against the pillow, her two brown braids disappearing beneath the quilt: looking from the back like a miniature grandmother.

I STOOD IN THE downtown library, looking at the long rows of books, trying to resist their lure. Certainly, I thought, here was one good way for a person to escape himself; it's as good as alcohol or drugs or sex or work. All you have to do is take one finger and pull out a volume and presto, you let the rest of the day take care of itself. And you do it neatly, painlessly; you can even pretend you are improving your mind. Pick a novel, any novel, and enter the ready-made world of Tolstoy or Arnold Bennett or Proust. You will soon think that you are thinking.

SIMENON MAKES THE simple, the ordinary, the everyday glow with the cool intensity of polished water glasses.

AT NINE O'CLOCK in the morning the neat-aproned, trim-bodied Mexican cook sings "Perfidia" as she bakes cookies for the noon meals. Soft, lilting words rise out of the shining pots and pans of the cafeteria.

YOU DRIFT ALONG, doing routinely this and that — possessing no real urgency or real desire — and then suddenly you find yourself genuinely hungry for a certain writer's world, his special mood and flavor. So you go once more to Graham Greene and his *Nineteen Stories,* or else follow the Chiapas mountain trails with his whiskey priest. Or remembering, and missing, the tone of "Disorder and Early Sorrow," you reread the first tales of Thomas Mann — or seek out again the lone figure of Steppenwolf. Maybe you want the spare dialogue of Hemingway people in Madrid; or Juan Ramon Jimenez telling Platero about twilight beauties of the Spanish countryside. Or perhaps nothing quite suits you except having midnight diner coffee with a couple of Steinbeck strikers.

That is always, to me, what good reading means: communing with a work and the man behind it. Some writers you cannot commune with; their words seem to be frozen within the type on the page. They are words produced by brains alone. That is why you read them and say, "My, that's fine," and then put the book away and never seek it out again. That is why you prefer reading the worst of a Sherwood Anderson to the best of a C. P. Snow.

A SMALL, LISTLESS school librarian sits at her desk in genuine boredom, a patch over one faulty eye. She looks as though a neatly printed card ought to be hanging around her neck: Beware The Nematode.

DOES THE INVISIBLE exist? The question is always before us. . . .

Yes, the Believers say: God is here and all-powerful; you just can't see Him.

No, say the Unbelievers, God is not here and never has been. I'll believe Him when I see Him.

Wellll, say the cautious middle-grounders, You-Just-Can't-Be-Sure.

There they are: the sides. The non-believers talk about the long history of man's superstition — his hailing of demons and gods in nature, his willingness to believe things which now, we know, are absurd. On the other hand the believers can point to the undeniable presence and power of the humanly unseeable: germs, atoms, electricity, gravity, the whole mysterious works.

So you keep on thinking: What will be accepted as *real* in another couple of thousand years? You look back on man's gradual discovery of his environment — and what can you say about *truth?* Has man been right or wrong in being awed, continuously, by the things he does not understand? What *is,* definitely, unchangeably, always; and what is *not?*

DURING MY YOUTH all the young men of talent were coming on like gangbusters, and all I could do was watch them, amazed. They acted like young gods, convinced they would never die.

SALESMAN AT REST: Pudgy-wristed, with fine, clean hairs lying on his hands. Neatly pressed green suit and polished brown loafers. Expensive watch and watchband catching the afternoon light that comes through the big cafe window. Tie still nicely knotted and just-slightly-beginning-to-thin brown hair still neatly combed.

He is drinking coffee at two in the afternoon, sitting in a side booth of the Oasis Cafe. The coffee is hot and the cafe is pleasantly air conditioned, but the salesman is not relaxed.

He lights a cigarette and blows smoke toward the window glass as he looks out at the cars passing in the street. He makes small movements of his mouth.

He is very clean. You can almost smell the after-shave lotion that he patted on his face in the early morning. His smoothly shaven chin is still shiny. Even his lower lip shines — but that is because of the taut dryness of his two o'clock soul.

Outside, the red light on the corner changes. Cars move forward again; sunlight glints from their roofs. The salesman stares through the glass, his legs crossed, the smoke from his cigarette hanging above his booth.

He doodles with his ballpoint on a note pad, making stars and rectangles and heavy underlinings of words. As each new customer comes into the cafe he glances up automatically, then sips again at his cup.

I cannot help but wonder: What thoughts are in his head as he outlines and re-outlines the stars on his notepad? What inner scenes does such a young man — a salesman for a roofing firm — visualize as he sits beside the big clear window, looking out? What are the concerns of his life that drift up from him, blurring, fading, like the smoke from his cigarette?

He remains there a while, an afternoon coffee drinker among many others — sunk into his deep personal cave. Then after selecting three nickels for a tip he rises, leaves the cafe, gets into his roofing car. He smooths his hair once with the flat of his hand, backs carefully away from the Oasis, disappears into the flow of sun-lit cars.

I THINK EVERY ADULT is close to tears — the tears he would shed if he ever paused long enough to confront, genuinely, the memory of himself as a child. They would not be tears of emotional release — of suddenly felt love or guilt or anger or self-pity. They would be, instead, tears of wrenching sadness, of profound loss. For as the adult confronted moments of the past — as he experienced once again the intensity of forgotten childhood moods and people and days — he would be overwhelmed by the mystery of human living, by the wonders of time and memory and change that could allow him to look, in his mind's eye, at the dim outline of his past self and still be that self in the present. . . . What was it like to be me then, the adult would ask; or, *Was* I really me, that long ago, in that shadowy place? And in asking he would perhaps understand a little more about the processes of life and death: about how the child he once was had died and yet had lived on.

. . . So it is: We lived so intimately there in the past, and then we left it, and forgot it, as though, indeed, we had never lived there at all; yet it remains, that strange and distant childhood, within us always — shaping our wishes, our fears, the very outline of our days.

I HAVE MANAGED to take perseverance, concern, and perception and mold them into a substitute for talent. It is as though, lacking genuine writing skills — the skills of a story teller — I have been able to function in writing by *desire alone*.

THE PUDGY P. E. teacher came up to me in the hall where I was on duty.

"I understand you are a writer," he said.

"Oh," I started out, "I try to do what I can whenever I —" I did not get very far.

"I've always thought *I'd* like to do some writing," he said, "if I could ever get around to it." His interruption was soft, unhurried, dreamlike, as though his mind was already caught up by an old familiar theme. As he talked he seemed to be gently unfocusing his eyes.

". . . I've had this story I've been thinkin' about now for a long time. It's about horses. You know there hasn't been a book on race horsin' since 1954. And there's been a lot of advances since that time, 'specially in drugs." He was smiling a little to himself as his thoughts began to warm.

DOODLEBUGS, and their smooth downward cone of almost silky dirt.

I THINK AND THINK and think and think, and nothing happens. I have a hopelessly dull mind.

THE BEST WORK done by American writers has generally been done at the first of their careers: this is now a truism. But *why* has this been the case? Some say that American writers just have one story to tell: the story of how they grew up and entered the Great World. But there is something else too. I think these writers, in the beginning, were writing only for themselves — out of their own deep enjoyments and concerns and perceptions. Then they were published and as a result got a public that "awaited their next work." The writers thereafter could not only not forget that public but unconsciously began to write *for* it.

To WRITE *for yourself alone* — that is the only way to stay in touch with poetry. Keep your words immensely personal. Never have the feeling that there is any kind of public looking over your shoulder — regardless of the times you have already published. *Do not think of the words you are writing as ever going into print.* If you write with the idea of communicating with others — as opposed to communicating with yourself — you lose the innocence of exploration and replace it with the dull, hard note of mere telling.

ALL AROUND HIM man was confronted with miracles. Some of these miracles he could solve, and he called his work with them Science. Others man could not solve, and he called these miracles Religion.

THE AFTERNOON IS my home; life is my business; thoughts are my children.

III

1967 - 1971

III

I HAVE ALREADY thought my main thoughts, and lodged my basic complaints. I guess I ought to stop writing.

READING CAN MAKE you a better editor, critic, psychologist, human being—but does it ever make you a better writer?

IT SEEMS NOW that my privateness, my anonymity, was my discipline, my cunning, my strength. Feeling utterly alone, I was able to keep a purity of purpose; I felt that I had an important, secret something to do.

THE PUBLIC SEEMS to use a convenient double standard when it considers creative people and their role in society. It does not, for example, *really* expect a violinist or a sculptor to be out on a civil rights picket line or to write stormy letters of protest to the local newspaper editor. The public takes for granted that such men lack the urge toward social involvement and thus are privileged, as Dedicated Artists, to be concerned only with their art.

But what about writers — artists in the use of words? Are they exempted too? Well, the public seems to say that poets are but that other writers are not. A poet — when he is thought of at all — is considered to be a person engaged in an intense and solitary pursuit of his muse, like the sculptor or painter; any other kind of writer is expected to be a citizen first and an artist secondly.

Think of it: according to the public, some men are obligated to have responsibilities to society and some are not. Some must respond to the body politic while others are to be purists following only the dictates and disciplines of their artistic specialty.

. . . Yet if you get down to practicalities, you discover that the public is not using double standards at all; it is just shrewd enough to realize that word-fashioners do not really have an audience and are of no consequence in national affairs. Thus the public is able to say, indulgently, "Sure, all right, go ahead and be Poets or Writers or whatever. Do what you please because . . . well, let's face it, you don't matter to us anyway. You've got no power, no influence; you're certainly not *dangerous* to anybody. So why shouldn't we let you pursue your butterflies of fancy. . . . Now and then, when times get slack, why, we can always remember that you guys are around, ready, for a couple of hours, to take people's minds off the practical business of living."

SOMEHOW THE SKETCH fits me. If I stop writing it, I am lost. . . . I will have to find a new means of approaching the days.

DAILY HUMAN PLEASURES help deny — up to a point — the ultimate human horrors.

I AM TEACHING at 3:15, standing before a class of failures. I have been talking quite a lot — hard, with genuine bursts of passion — and have been able to get the class to talking some too. They are a discouraged and discouraging lot, for the most part, yet just for this brief span of time it seems that the artificial structures of the room have fallen away and we are simply gathered together to talk things over: students and a teacher linked only by circumstance yet for a few moments genuinely exposed to one another.

As I stand before them, very tired, ready for the school day to end, a curious thing happens. A sudden emotion surges through me, and I find that I am saying to myself, "Why, I love these people."

It has happened before like this: being around the weak-eyed, the down-and-out, and suddenly — because I had come to know a little about the hidden shapes of their lives — feeling a great respect for them and then a sense of love.

. . . I look out at those in English IIM, just as the bell rings, and all I can see is their humanness: they hurt, they are vulnerable and unsure, they have had a rough go of things. But for a while their defenses have been down, and for the better part of an hour they have been sitting here as rather pleasant folks, really; rather ordinary human flesh.

WHITE SUBURBAN AMERICANS talk about the meaninglessness of life in general; black ghetto Americans talk about the meaninglessness of their lives specifically. Surely this provides *some* common ground for dialogue. . . .

WALKING UNDER TREES in New Braunfels:
It was an exquisite pain, that loneliness of my twenties. I did not think I would survive it. Alone — with no place that was specially mine, with no sense of a calling in life — I walked at night under street lights and tall green trees. I listened as I walked, and heard nothing important.

A terrible time, full of self and a free-floating pain. At twenty-five I had rejected much; little remained for me to turn to. I had only the night, the trees, the great dark silence: — and houses, where people slept contentedly with wives and children and furniture; and streets, where people in the daylight hours went back and forth to jobs that kept them tied to life.

I walked under the huge trees, hearing my footsteps on the sidewalk. Porches loomed silently within the yards. There were crickets and tree frogs and katydids, all pulsing in the darkness. No dogs barked, no idle sighs escaped through the open summer windows. At midnight it was just me, moving through quiet neighborhoods — aimless under the pecans and sycamores.

THE SHOCK, and exquisite sadness, of discovering, at 17, that you have a past.

THE SOUTH: a place of Negroes and great human wrongs.

Yet I wonder: Is it conceivable that some of the inexcusable acts of men against men could have been balanced somewhat by the healing powers of nature — by the sheer presence of woods and rivers and silence and animals moving quietly through tall grasses? Did men, both black and white, survive there with more grace than an outsider would think was possible?

THE THINGS which are emotionally meaningful for me are, by any enlightened person's standards, reactionary and hopelessly square. But since my emotions are not governed by my intellect, I remain true to my childhood and the world I knew as I lived within it: the faces, songs, and life styles of the Texas hill country.

I can see, therefore, why Faulkner was such an apologist for Mississippi: he simply couldn't help himself. His mind, which rejected Mississippi's faults, was no match for his emotions, which embraced what *was* instead of what should have been.

IT IS OF NO INTEREST to simply sit down and write about what you already know. You might as well type names out of a telephone directory or post figures in a bank. Writing is suddenly having a mood, a scene, a vision from the past to rise slowly in a far part of your mind like a porpoise or some sporting fish lazily taking the air in a tranquil bay, remaining arced there in a frozen moment of time and space, and then slicing back into the bland covering of water from which it came.

Writing, to be in the least exciting or interesting, must not be just a skillful *putting down* but an earnest *straining after,* a *trying to catch,* a grasping toward something that suddenly seems to have a beauty and a wholeness and a setting — a something that you have actually known quite well for a long while but which never before had shook away all its excess. That's what causes the sudden urgency, the delight: realizing that something intimate is flashing majestically upward out of the depths of experience and is going to expose itself fully for a moment in the present light before easing down again to its old shadowed bed.

A HUMAN BEING simply cannot deal with ultimates. He can ignore them, camouflage them, laugh at them, distort them, but he cannot *accept* them.

BEAUTY AND THE BEAST: People feel better when they see cripples with redeeming features: the paraplegic with a good sense of humor; the cerebral palsied child with a high intelligence; the deaf, one-armed boy with great athletic skill.

And of course a blind street singer should always have a beautiful voice.

But Eugenio, who is blind and enormously fat, has a rasping, tuneless, ugly voice. Each afternoon during the summer he sits on Sixteenth of September Street in Juarez, across from Our Lady of Guadalupe cathedral, and makes loud cheerless noises. He sits on a stool with his legs spread apart and sings his songs and it is as though a very dull needle, placed on a warped and worn-out record, is creating sound through a loudspeaker with loose connections. Eugenio, sweating even in the shade, bawls out his songs toward the invisible cathedral and the invisible people moving by — his mouth wide open, showing his rotting teeth; his eyes wobbling about in their wrinkled sockets.

And standing next to him each afternoon is a very pretty little girl. She comes out of a dress shop two doors down the sidewalk and takes up her waiting position there beside him. It is as if Eugenio is a handsome operatic tenor and she is his modest lady-in-waiting. She listens patiently, attentively, her large dark eyes never seeming to blink as she gazes out toward the hot afternoon. Eugenio bellows, strikes clumsy chords on his old guitar, rolls his clotted, marble eyes. The child stands quietly beside him, very thin and pretty, listening closely to his anguished cries.

TODAY'S CHILDREN grow up surrounded by other children; I grew up surrounded by trees.

What happens if you relate as much to nature as you do to people? Do you learn not to hunt for all your satisfactions in human sources? If you once find how to get pleasure out of a riverbank, how frustrated do you become later on when you discover that society — its laws, its governings — is less than perfect?

IT IS TOO BAD that people who live next to the land, who plant fruit trees, raise goats and sheep, work with their hands in the sun, cultivate potatoes and beans and squash, drink water from their own wells, bake pies and shell pecans, love horses and border collies and grandchildren, sit before fireplaces on winter nights, milk cows and churn butter, take afternoon naps and sit after dark on quiet front porches — it is too bad that such people, who lead such enviable and contenting lives, are not always enviable as human beings.

WHAT IS THE GESTALT of me? Where do I extend, invisibly?

. . . Sometimes, in a moment of great privateness, I can almost perceive that I do not end with my body, with my apparent limitations, but that I am *open*, somehow — capable of a larger sense of self and being.

Yet the moment is brief, and before it reveals a deeper extension of me-into-It, the outside fades away. I am once more quite familiarly me.

Do I merely inhabit this body for a while, and then does it merely cease its curious functioning? Or am I more than the sum of my parts: do I function *in relation to,* infinitely?

IN THE NEXT BLOCK a deep-throated dog keeps calling the afternoon into account — keeps challenging his dog-universe like a lone Greek god bellowing into the silence of antiquity.

I DO NOT UNDERSTAND fall silences. I walk into the bathroom and hear an emptiness there that I did not hear all summer long. I stand for a moment, listening, and it is as though God had at last deserted the earth — had finally withdrawn the last echo of himself and disappeared from the universe.

TO WRITE IS to remain integrated.

OCTOBER, MONTH OF MOODS. . . . Suddenly there are new October ways to see and hear; October silences and shadows. Rock walls, sides of houses, doorways, posts: in October they stand private, isolated, self-absorbed — like stilled animals listening to the faint sounds of approaching winter.

YOU KNOW, I ACCEPT the unfathomable mysteries of space, the tragic cast of all human experience, the ultimate question mark of life — but let me also say this: One night I went into the bedroom of my five-year-old daughter and lay my face close to hers as she slept; I listened to her, breathing and sighing in that semi-dark room; I looked at the lovely, satisfying curve of her neck and cheek; I all but tasted the sweet-flavored childish essence that seemed to emanate from her body. And so satisfying was she to look at, and touch, and consider — such a *gift* she was, deep within her covers, with her soft, glowing skin and good-smelling hair — that I could not help but say to the nothingness as I left her room: Good-God-a-mighty. . . .

I GROPED ABOUT, fashioning my Notebook and Sketch the way another might fashion his Crutch or Sword.

I AM TRYING to make experience *mean* something again. That is, I've been experiencing experience so long now that I can't seem to react to it any more the way I should — the way I want to. It's like having the juice go out of the Juicy Fruit when you still have the gum in your mouth — except that is not a good analogy, for *life* does not lose its flavor; rather, I suppose I have lost part of the capacity to savor, or the willingness to savor, or maybe even the need to savor.

I'm thinking mainly about sensory pleasures: about the early Camus sun-on-the-body and blue-waters-beyond-the-sand Algerian pleasures; the pleasures that every young body feels and then translates to the mind as being good. Because with me body-pleasures stimulate the mind to do *its* work. The body, the earth, sensory things: they are primary, and if they say Life loud enough, then writing seems to come almost as a natural consequence, in reflex.

I try to fight this lessening of verve, of glad reaction, but will power alone is never any good in trying to whip up joy. And it is joy, celebration, that should be the goal in writing: the passionate response to life, delivered in the full knowledge of death and chaos: the careful, *human* reaction, with as much body involved as brain.

. . . This joy business: what Norman Brown was getting at in *Life Against Death*: the pleasure of existing in the world, of playing in it. But god-in-heaven, who can play much right now, in this time of Vietnam, without somehow being able to wall off part of your awareness. . . . Yet perhaps that is part of the New Challenge: saying despite it all, despite the slowing down of the body and the frustrating times, you must celebrate; you must learn how to fight back against public and private despair.

YOU ARE READING on a quiet Sunday afternoon. For a while the only sounds you hear are familiar ones of the house — the clock ticking in the kitchen, a window pane rattling from a rising breeze. It is a commonplace stretch of time, satisfying in its emptiness.

Then, as if all perceptible winds of the earth had suddenly stilled, you hear a sound from the yard that makes you lower your book in awe. You begin to stare vaguely into space, murmuring, "It has been so long. . . ." It is as though you are hearing a familiar memory moving around out there, some free and contented part of your former self that had long ago slipped quietly out of your life and into the world.

The sound is really nothing at all. Perhaps only the neighbor boy talking in his high-pitched voice, telling his father about a cat that has climbed into a cottonwood tree. Perhaps it is a dog barking somewhere down the street — just an ordinary dog barking at some ordinary four o'clock object. Perhaps it is a slow airplane going by overhead, or a man sawing a board in his driveway.

The sound itself is not important; it is the stretch of utterly vacant time in which it occurs — the narrow corridor in a Sunday afternoon which allows a simple sound to be heard intact, with all its echoes. It is that rare moment when, if a bell should ring, it would seem not to be ringing from a church down the street but from some belfrey of eternity.

MICROCOSM: A man stands looking at a willow sapling on an early spring morning — hands in his pockets, bending forward from the waist a little as he peers closely for a sign of greenery. He lives on a slope of the Franklin Mountains and from his front yard he can look out across flat desert lands to the horizon — literally, to the end of the earth.

This bending, squinting man does not know if he is upside down, in relation to Venus, or right side up, in relation to Mars. Such things are not his concern and he would be the first to tell me so if I walked over into his yard. He is a human being, a citizen and home owner of El Paso, Texas, and that is quite sufficient for him. Earth, Mars, the universe — all of God's marvelous Tinker Toys: Why, he knows they exist, of course, but so what? There is certainly nothing he can do about them. They are not fit subjects for a person's thoughts. But a tree, now, beginning to bud — that's different. That's something a man can get up close to and touch: something he can understand.

THERE ARE TALKERS of words; then there are writers of them. Talkers can be writers, of course, but generally they are not.

A talker achieves release and ego-satisfaction only if another person is there being impressed by his words; he does not have the opportunity for that same kind of release when he faces a blank sheet of paper: the uncertainties which he feels within himself cannot be buried beneath the steady sound of his self-hypnotizing voice.

MY WHOLE LIFE is simply a debt to be paid. The problem is how to pay it, and to whom.

I THINK ON PAPER; I do not create.

I HAVE IN ME the Loch Ness monster of easy sentiment. Frequently it emerges, moaning, from the swirling deep of Frank Sinatra-and-Eddie-Arnold tunes and makes it way toward the bare Scotlandic coastline of my emotions.

MEXICO IS MEDIEVAL in its *acceptance* of the way life is. It accepts good and bad, health and suffering, rich and poor. (Where is compassion? That is not just a Protestant or modern luxury. . . .)

SHERWOOD BEFORE BREAKFAST: I have been reading Sherwood Anderson before breakfast. I read about driven men who write beautiful imaginary novels on park benches, men who go off to other towns just to walk around there and savor the town's strangeness — to feel alone and anonymous; men who go down to New Orleans and meet other men — small aristocratic Southern poets who limp and drink because of the wounds of World War I.
Some of the stories I read are little more than incidents and remembrances, but I don't mind. I read the second-rate right along with his best because I am not looking for perfection out of Sherwood Anderson. I don't read him in the early morning for that. What I go to his books for is the sense of life, of old mysterious mortality, of how it is to be human and alive and mov-

ing about on the earth — especially, moving about with a little imagination.

Thus we manage to establish a friendly communion, this man and I. He is not like so many writers who take pains to hide themselves carefully behind the shining machinery of their words. He stands there in full view, in all his apparent artlessness: a writing man, loose on the world with his senses intact; a man with regions of America, and the regions' people, inside his head — a man who wants to tell about them compassionately, and with wonder.

WOMAN ON THE RIDGE: when I left the house at dusk the sky was still overcast, but the rain of the afternoon had stopped. I had no place to go and no thoughts to think so I drove the streets aimlessly. Finally I stopped at the long scenic ridge that overlooks the heart of town. I cut off the motor and began to stare out into space — letting my mind enter into the moodiness of the damp afternoon.

As I sat there, brooding, I noticed a woman walking on the sidewalk along the rim, slowly coming my way. She looked Jewish and reflective — perhaps a middle-aged widow out for a walk at the end of the day, gazing down toward the red-brick buildings that had been darkened by the rain. She was short, rather fleshy, with pleasantly full hips. . . .

I began to wonder what the woman would do when she passed my car. Was she so absorbed in her thoughts that she wouldn't even bother to notice solitary cars along the ridge — or would she be mildly curious and steal a glance? Was it possible, even, that she would not only look at the car but would try to see who the driver was inside and perhaps form some kind of opinion of him?

I waited, and as she came idling past — pretending to be looking straight ahead — I caught her glancing briefly at my hand resting on the back of the seat. Since I was holding a pencil, and there were books scattered in the back, she probably decided I was not any kind of threat: a young-looking man parked at the edge of a bluff at sunset, holding a pencil, with books about —surely that kind of evidence was enough to make me a student rather than a solitary drinker or a rapist. . . .

I watched her continue along the rim. I liked the way she walked, the slow, meditative gait. . . . Did she perhaps own one of the big double-decker mansions nearby — one with a sweeping view of the city and sculptured greenery and lombardy poplars: Was she a woman-with-everything out seeking answers to the emptiness of her life?

I watched her disappear around a curve and then I started the car and drove away — wondering what she would have done, that short, well-hipped, reflective, Jewish-looking woman, if suddenly I had gotten out of the car — if I had called out loudly but politely, "Oh, ma'am . . . ma'am" — and then casually began to lope after her, my student-like demeanor serving as a badge of my good intentions. As she stood half-paused, half-turned, would she have thought that I was Fate running toward her along that gray, darkening ridge — a latter-day Thomas Wolfe ready to astound and enmesh his Esther Jack with a net of romantic, besieging, redeeming words?

IF THERE WERE no life in the world, would life *necessarily* have to be created? Would a universe without life be as "important" as one with it?

WE DELIGHT IN every variety of nature except human. We marvel at flamingos, Grand Canyons, zebras, pyramids, boa constrictors, yet we are immensely critical of people who are not Exactly Like Us.

CRITICS CAN TEAR a lousy book to pieces. They feel helpless and confused, however, when faced with something good — indeed, even feel resentful toward the author for having done *his* job so well that *they* are left with nothing to do except offer praise.

MOST PEOPLE do a thing because they *know* that thing. With me, this is not the case. Once I know something it no longer interests me; the magic of discovery has disappeared. (It would bore me to death to be an "authority.")

That is why teaching — the more or less constant repetition of what I already know — often becomes intolerable, and why writing keeps luring me on. For in writing, your job is always that which has never been done before. It's like being a Father-God and perpetually creating Man: first you find the germ, the stuff of an individual life; then you must give shape and substance; finally you must set your creation on his own two feet. If he is truly a man, if he truly exists, then he will be autonomous from you and your job is over. You don't become an "authority" on him; he becomes his own authority on himself. So you just leave him and move along — trying to be ready for that next germ, that next creation.

WRITING IS TAKING the shadows formed by the fires on earth and projecting them into a second, even more compelling reality.

IT'S LIKE BEING a church organ, yet every day having to make the sounds of a dog whistle.

IF I WERE a genius I would be working furiously, until I dropped. The urgency that would keep welling up from knowing and feeling and understanding would be so overwhelming that I would drive myself to the wall in the sweet agony of creation.

READING BORGES on a June Day: I look out into the street, to the glare of three o'clock, and it is business-as-usual. Trucks lumber by, going west; car brakes squeal; buildings loom impersonally. Bareheaded, frowning men walk slowly in the sun, trying to hitch rides.

Yet inside the waiting room of the old train station the light is subdued and the air is calm — quite suitable for reading Borges. The many empty benches and the high somber roof seem to encourage a casual look into memories.

I turn the pages of this curious man — so full of the sadness and poetry of long living — as he winds his way through history, pauses, deliberates, finds his labyrinth, his mirror, his irony, moves on. I move with him, ready to consider his question or share his mood.

Yet suddenly, without knowing why, I find that I am no longer walking the side streets of Buenos Aires but instead am looking at agarita bushes full of red berries, and the long leaves of mesquites, and a stretch of hill country road lying in the glare of summer midday. For a moment I am gazing past the lowered book into a scene of my childhood.

This intruding recollection loses its power, fades, and I am once again sitting beside the waiting room door, with Borges. But the magic of reflection is not easily undone. Borges, berries — I begin to marvel at how simply the gap was spanned between his memories and mine. . . .

I look down. His dreams — those unreal realities which so often have been his despair — are fixed substantially to the page. He molded them, finally, into the iron shape of words.

Yet what about my own pampas, I wonder, and the Argentine-like sunlight of my own past: He can never tell me anything of them. That delicate, probing finger which has sampled the winds blowing across his life and thoughts — it can never sample mine.

I rise, go to the doorway with the book under my arm. As I squint into the glare and watch the trucks go by, I think: Yes, of course, read Borges, salute him — but then move on. Do not linger within his spell too long. . . . Every memory has its master; your memories are your own to tame.

I WRITE NOW, but with a lack of urgency. At 37 I do not

feel there are any private truths left to discover, any personal reve-
lations still to be made. I have lapsed into an acceptance of the no-
answers in life — a deadly pseudo-serenity that provides neither
wisdom nor a sense of peace.

A PERSON ALWAYS feels emptiest when he is full of passions but has no outlet for them.

ONE BECOMES HIMSELF not by having perfect freedom but
by being *in opposition to, in relation to, in contrast to.* Only when
there is a strong not-you are you forced to become strongly yourself.

PERSONAL TRUTHS are like tough desert seeds. They lie
buried, unseen, beneath the dry sands of 'daily living; yet given
even the least watering, by accident, they spring alive with their
old stunning glory.

WHAT OUR BODY responds to, our mind delights in.

THE INTELLECT, by itself, is as awesome and lonely as a
universe without God.

THIS BRIGHT, cool, '68 generation: they are sure of themselves; they feel they are pure. They see ideals sharply — but not
life or human nature.

I HAD BEEN SITTING at my desk, typing along, convincing
myself that I was involved in meaningful work, when after a bit
I leaned back in my chair, folded my hands — and happened to
look into my lap. There, like a gently wagging finger of God, was
the pulse in my left wrist, throbbing serenely.
I was shocked and embarrassed — for not two feet away the
mystery of life was obviously mocking me and my High Serious-

ness — and I wanted to respond in some way to the pulse: wanted to call down awkwardly and say, BUT I HAVEN'T THOUGHT ABOUT YOU IN MONTHS.

. . . There it was, banging away softly, loyally, beneath my skin, keeping me alive for every hour of every day while I, in the splendid provincialism of my ego-world, could forget that my pulse beat even existed.

LIFE TIRES US unless we can be rejuvenated daily by simplicities.

IT'S A NEW EXISTENCE to look and not feel, to see and not react.

DUSK, and I walked along the back streets of downtown El Paso where Mexican families lived in small, red-brick apartments. The day was ending quietly, and the faint smell of brake fluid from a neghborhood garage hung in the air like a pleasant evening perfume of the poor.

Through the window of a small corner grocery store I could see a young girl in a pink sweater: she was leaning forward on the counter, talking to a boy eating candy, and her back made a peaceful curve in the dim grocery store light.

I passed a window where an old woman sat in her small, carefully cluttered room under a yellow bulb. A parrot was rocking in his cage. A home altar was on a table against the wall.

As I moved along in my isolation, in the cold late-afternoon, it was almost as if I had become my own priest and were walking down the aisles of my own red-brick temple of humanity.

A SMALL DECEMBER COINCIDENCE: It is a very cold afternoon in Juarez and a man is walking along carrying a long board. He has on an old black hat and a black coat and black shoes. Beside him, holding his free hand, walks his small son, who is wearing a black coat and worn-out shoes.

They are moving steadily along, in the severe cold, and they have come to a street corner where a group of boys are playing soccer at the bottom of a rocky hill. At the corner the man, without breaking the rhythm of his walk, jumps across a wide mud puddle with his son and his board.

Nearby, all the while, in a small bare elm tree, there has been a sparrow. It has been sitting on a limb. And as the man holds his son's hand, and his board, and jumps, the sparrow, at the same moment, stirs itself from its limb and jumps also — to another nearby limb.

The man continues his sober, dogged walk up the hill. The group of barefooted boys continue to chase after their soccer ball. The sparrow sits on its new limb, hunched once more in the cold.

STANDING AT DUSK in December beside an old barn — on a cold, deserted, and dying ranch — and thinking of a title that Thomas Hardy might have used and gotten away with: "In the Lee of the Winds of Time."

MAE, REMEMBERED: At 11:30 and 5:00 each day except Sunday I could back off from my college despairs into table-waiting routines at the boarding house. I could slice lemons and fix pitchers of tea and carry out bowls of rice and carrots and peas to the tables and then, when the doors opened, I could stand at the back of the dining room in my white apron and look out across the heads of future engineers and drama majors and fraternity boys and be rather content.

Thirty minutes before the evening meal I would take my apron off the hook behind the hall door and, whistling, begin to lay out plates in the dining room. Mae would be limping around in the kitchen — checking rolls in the oven, washing pans, wiping sweat, sweet-Jesusing at all the work that still needed to be done before five-thirty. After I would pour up the ketchup and get out the jelly and butter and set the silverware and napkins beside the plates, I would come back to the kitchen doorway and, leaning against it, pretend to drum my foot. Mae — usually washing a pot at the sink, her arms deep in suds — would turn and slide a look towards me. Then she would stop washing and let her big-lipped grin make its way out of the sweat and meaty blackness of her face: "Shi-it, Leroy," she would say, her words exploding a little, her head dropping forward. She stayed that way a moment, shaking her head from side to side before throwing back her head in a long, throat-throbbing laugh. It was the laugh of an always fat, always tired colored woman (— still Colored, then, in the '50s, not Black): a fat colored woman looking over at a skinny white college-kid in tennis shoes and thinking that he meant no harm of course but that he didn't know his ass from a water pitcher when it came to understanding how an East Austin cook felt in a white woman's kitchen in the late afternoon of an ordinary work day.

But for both of us I think it was a pleasant communication and release: that head-shake, that look, that laugh, in that quiet, 5:20 house.

BEYOND EVERY STREET CORNER is the sky. Beyond every voice is silence. Beyond every passion is disenchantment.

BETWEEN BUSES the waiting room is empty except for a few regulars hunched over on the benches. They come in to get out of the cold, to be where people are, to talk to themselves, to doze. They are tolerated by the management — no one ever tries to run them out. As they sit, motionless in their worn-out shoes and ragged coats, they are like charter members of the Lost-and-Forlorn Club.

. . . This old Mexican man and I: We were partners. Each night he sits here on the bench, slumped to one side, smelling of Vicks salve and month-old sweat. The black mole on his temple is hidden beneath his hunting cap, his mouth sags with each private snore.

Another Mexican man wearing cement-stained shoes, with tattoos on his forearms, sighs loudly into the stillness. "Oh, my *good*-ness,' he says, and the words are almost lyrical, like the beginning of a prayer or very sad song.

Two small men, both looking slightly Oriental, sit together and smile toward each other from time to time. One gently digs the other in the ribs as they quietly talk. Both seem rather sly, as if they are able to live satisfactorily on just the margins of life. The more passive man picks up the loose cover of a comic book from the floor, handles it delicately, turns it about, spends a long time looking it over carefully. It is obvious he can make do with what others throw away.

STYLE REFLECTS the shape a writer's personality has taken after he has twisted about here and there, trying to find the most comfortable position in which to survive.

ALL RIGHT, accept the reality of your condition instead of lamenting it. Accept the fact that basically your writing is simply You-Alone in some situation: you in a bar, looking; you on a street, searching; you in a country place, reacting. In your writing you are simply talking to the paper about all the things you have seen and felt *while alone*; about all the little moments of intensity, *while alone*. That's the title of your work: *Me: Alone: in the World: Looking.*

IF I WERE a painter I would probably drive myself nuts trying to capture, say, how it is when a group of school kids stand together at noon, talking, rather subdued but still self-possessed, facing more or less toward each other in a circle, with the midday sun streaming down across their faces. . . . It would be the meeting of the sun and their faces that I would be trying to capture. I would want the paint brush to do the impossible task of suggesting, somehow, not just sunlight but history, and youth, and timelessness, and time passing, and the valuableness of a single moment of human living.

Such a wash of possibilities was there yesterday when I looked at a group in the sun: students, -paused, -in-the-sun-streaming: a poem of flesh-in-light.

A WRITER IS a cripple who uses words as sutures to bind together the fractures of his life.

. . . A PERSON DOES, a person is, but he cannot be "written about." A person moves tenuously among monstrous unknowns — within him and without. A person is a One — just that: a singularity among many. His life is like a hidden lake — constantly seeping to other places, a formless moving of life obeying unfelt gravities and pressures: a reservoir of potentials, created mysteriously and always mysteriously leaking back to its unknown sources.

WHAT USED TO BE the supreme moment of American youth: the night of high school graduation. In the space of a single hour you crested the Continental Divide of adolescence and started the long journey down toward the hidden, opposite sea.

. . . You listened to the sounds of symphonic music and expected life to reflect, later, those impressive sounds: *Pomp and Circumstance,* and *Recessional,* with graduates coming down the dusty middle aisle of the open-air auditorium, mortar boards wobbling, bodies encased in strange black gowns.

You expected life to be what that slow, throat-swelling sentimental music suggested that life *must* be: a long passing through Colorado-like territory, with pine-covered mountains all around, ringed with clouds and snow and technicolored promises.

THE ONLY Work-in-Progress I have to offer is my life.

ONE CAN WRITE of the particular, the local, the individualized, but he must do it with the sense of revealing the cosmic, the unending, the all. . . .

One must deal with the totality of living, which includes nonliving; with everything that is and was; with China and bones in the ground and mosquito bites and galaxies expanding.

AT 18 EVERYTHING MATTERS. At 28 certain things matter. At 38 a few things matter.

At 48 — will anything matter?

DO WE LIVE TOO LONG? Once enthusiasm, and innocence, and hope are gone, what is left — except seeing the birth and gradual death of those same capacities in your own children?

THE KNOWLEDGES THAT come with sunset; the joys that come with morning.

IS IT POSSIBLE to write stories now? Have social and political involvements — concern for national goals, national values — become so overriding that imaginative re-creations of life are considered irrelevant? Is this the Reportorial Age, brought about by subtle pressures from television to be *current*? Has Mailer found himself, finally, because he does so perfectly what the times demand? (Who remembers Thomas Wolfe with Tom Wolfe around?)

. . . Who, indeed, is writing stories in Texas today? Novels — yes; they are still being done. But the Katherine Anne Porter kind of short fiction: is that over? Does the present belong now to the article-writers, the sociologists, and the alienated? And is the past slipping back into the hands of historians, folklorists, regionalists?

How avante-garde it would be for some young fellow in Round Rock or Halletsville to say to himself, in 1970: By George, you know what I think I'll do; I think I will sit down and write about those people I knew, in that place, in that summer afternoon. I think I'll try to write me a *story*. . . .

THESE UNDER-30 FOLKS who act as though they are *passing judgment* when they refer to the Old. They seem to think that aging is not simply a fact of life but is, instead, some kind of betrayal by the unenlightened. They act as if their own youth was arrived at by a superior insight — as if they are a breed conceived outside normal biological processes and thus are destined to live forever in a state of beauty and grace.

I AM ON THE opposite side of the fence from critics because, as intellectuals, they are primarily interested in literature — in words.

I am on the side of the writers, who are not interested, basically, in words: they are concerned with experience, with people and happenings of the world. They go to words only as a last resort — in an attempt to present life, as they have felt it, to others. Thus they go to literature by way of life; intellectuals go directly to words — reading them, mouthing them — and many times never get around to life at all.

RITUALS FINALLY BECOME the saving grace of one's life. They begin to please at the time when other things begin to lose their flavor. The body, beginning its gradual winding down due to stiff joints and uncooperative muscles, welcomes comfortable places in which it can sink.

THIS MORNING, between eight and nine, I watched my children playing on the living room rug. The room was still rather dark, the record player was on, and the two of them were spraddle-legged on the floor — Deborah, 7, and Byron, not yet one year old.

I watched, and listened, and smiled, and knew that I would never find any other moment in life more satisfying, more touched with grace.

I SEE JODL walking out of the train station at five-fifteen, a folded newspaper in his hand. I watch him stride through the wide front door and across the cement porch and onto the sidewalk. As he moves along beside the high rock wall that hides the tracks, I glance above the wall and see, on the rise of ground that begins Sunset Heights, the old two-story buildings that have faced into Mexico since the turn of the century.

I sit on my bench inside the station, thinking: Yes, there he is. Jodl is passing by again at five-fifteen, just as he has done so many afternoons before, and it is all quite ordinary. Cars are parked out front, as usual; the air is warm, as August air is supposed to be. The street sounds of trucks passing, cab doors slamming — they are routine and familiar. It is all so typical this afternoon, so —

And immediately the other, more awesome word is there: . . . so *timeless*. Timeless as the old house on the hill, as Mexico across the Rio Grande.

I continue to watch Jodl moving toward town in his slow, rearing-back way — passing now through the station's shadow that is thrown on the wall, now through bright sunlight — yet it is as if he is walking against the backdrop of Every Afternoon, Every Day. . . . And I begin to wonder: How was it fifty years ago for a man to leave this same station at this same time of day, carrying his daily newspaper? And how will it be fifty years from now? Does sunlight, the shadow of a building — the very air — change from year to year, century to century? If I could have seen a man walking toward his home in Pompeii — just before the lava and ashes came pouring down — would it have been the same as watching Jodl go into the street just now?

. . . How much does the *feel* of life change — and how much does it stay the same?

SLIM, PLEASANT, balding men walk along beside their very pretty wives. . . .

How do such men manage to hold such women?

The women — their hair softly bouncing, their complexion

looking flawless, their trim bodies sheathed inside tailored slacks and fuzzy sweaters: they are indisputable knockouts. They are stunning young matrons loaded with cool-and-collected sex appeal.

How do these serious-faced, deferential bald-heads in their wash-and-wear pants and Saturday-morning loafers manage to keep the little women in tow? And why do the women seem so genuinely content? . . . Is it that constant reassuring male hand at the elbow? or that dutifully turned head? Or is it merely the quiet, steady air of the husband that says: Darling, I will work every day at my $30,000-a-year job — for our children, our summer home in Cloudcroft, and your trim little tail. . . .

FARM ROAD TO Old Mesilla: I drive slowly, letting the fields and distant mountains have their say. I am in no hurry. I am made content by the countryside.

Passing a canal I see a woodpecker hanging upside down from a cottonwood. The smooth feathers of its head are like a gray stocking pulled exquisitely tight — with holes cut for its small, glass-like eyes. It looks out at me through the broad leaves of the tree and does not move.

Over there, on the right, a small garden lies in the noontime sun. A quiet place, not too self-important. . . . But beyond its fence a lane runs underneath many elm trees, and there is a pleasant, jagged path of filtered sun that stretches narrowly down the center: a fuse of light burning toward the horizon.

On the left there are pumps, plows, trucks. They look strong and friendly — like silent testimonials for the dignity of work and the sanity of the earth. Behind them, scattered columns of dust and smoke rise against the long slope of a mountain range.

Occasionally there are neatly plowed fields — designs left on a draftsman's huge brown board — and arroyos bordered with green willows, their flat beds full of sand and gravel washed clean by summer rains.

And every so often there are the small houses of Mexican families sitting beside fields of corn. They are like calm outposts along the grim frontier of modern life.

THIS IS A TIME when you can easily be a young person of great style and beauty, if not substance. Today, stance is everything. (Yet we forget, as we get older, that the only real possession a young person has is his body. Thus it is natural that he often displays it, decorates it, defends it, uses it — aggressively.)

THE LONG, aimless years of my past: I consider them, and they seem formless, stupidly pursued (This curious prejudice for the present: As you glance backwards the whole past course of events, in its innocence of *now,* seems wholly ineffectual, lacking in direction and grace.)

ALL OF US LONERS know the good public places.

A WRITER'S self-confidence always hovers close to zero because no matter what he has ever done he must do it again, for one creative act demands another, and another, and another. . . .

IN JUAREZ on a summer day: For a long while I had sat in Benito Juarez Plaza,, resting among the pigeon droppings and dozing old men. The three o'clock air was heavy and still. Then, like strange scattered birds coming slowly, relentlessly, through the plaza trees, the distant cries of the newsboys began to float my way:
"Mexi . . . canoooooooohhh. Mexi . . . canoooooooohhh."
The cries plummeted, faded; finally small barefoot boys came hurrying past the benches selling "El Mexicano." Their hair gently flopping, they watched for a nod, a sign, the newspaper ready in their hand as they moved past. Soon men in straw hats, with sacks of newspapers slung across their shoulders, strode in from the other side of the plaza, their own mild cries lifted into the heat and the sidewalk elms.
"Mexi . . . canoooooooohhh. Mexi . . . canoooooooohhh."
I bought a paper, folded it, started to read, then began watching a young man who was sporting around with members of his pack in the center of the plaza. His eyes were sunk in a morass of dark

eyebrows and dark eyelashes, his Roman nose profiled strongly, his huge, perfect bow of mouth framed white, even teeth — making him look like a caramel-skinned Francis X. Bushman. His shirt hung loose and unbuttoned down the front, and when he moved about the shirt flew open, showing purple circles around his nipples and his flat stomach with its huge protruding navel.

He could not keep his hands off the boys in his gang. With shoulder shoves, arm blows, thumb-and-forefinger shakings of an underling's neck, he remained in a steady mock-fight: testing their willingness to let him be their bullyboy. Grinning, posturing, whirling, egging-on, he teemed with sensual aggressiveness.

As I got up from my bench to leave, an American tourist in a blue yachting cap and plaid walking shorts strolled down the sidewalk. Two Tarahumara Indians — babies strapped on their backs, barefooted — stepped out in front of him to beg. They thrust their faces upward toward the man, pleading with high, intense, wailing voices — and at the first negative shake of the man's head they hushed. They began and ended their cries so flatly, so abruptly, it seemed as if a door to some Room of Ageless Laments had suddenly come ajar and just as suddenly had been slammed shut.

*

I left the plaza, still seeking something deeper of the afternoon, of Mexico, of myself.

I walked until I came to a deserted vendor's stand in a dusty vacant lot. I sat in the shade of the stand, listening to a tractor working behind me in a blocked-off street. The smell of dust and tar was in the air, and somewhere close by, in a bar, ranchero music played on a juke box — slow and steady and loud.

As I glanced about, restlessly, I saw that just within the shade of the stand lay a cluster of bones. They were so smoothly coated with oil and dust they seemed to be wearing smooth dark fur. I kept looking at them, wondering whether you could always tell if a bone were human or not. . . .

Old cars kept bumping along across the vacant field, detouring around the barracaded street behind me. Heads of children rocked gently in the back seats, like heads at sea, as the cars swayed through the dusty ruts. Once two barefooted girls hurried along, carrying a block of ice in a bucket between them. They smiled when they saw me, giggled, then had to stop and get a new grip on the bucket.

When I got up to leave I noticed two trees, tall and white-barked, standing at opposite ends of a long pink building at the other end of the field. The building itself seemed very much a part of the afternoon — flushed and forlorn, intimidated by heat, having an almost womanly look of wan disenchantment. But the trees were aloof from it, like aristocrats. They not only seemed to be privately enduring the last dog days of summer but were actually managing to surmount them. Bent slightly toward each other, they appeared to be nodding courtly Spanish greetings to one another: *salud*, they seemed to be saying across the dust and emptiness and dry August heat.

EXPERIENCE, OF COURSE, is simply chaos presented in a straight line.

IN THE MUSEUM: Grinning skulls from centuries past; the long, silent rooms; and the Sunday visitors who wander about casually *and are not overwhelmed.*

I WILL BE very old — wrinkled, sightless, hard of hearing — and a young man will ask, a bit shyly, what I had learned during my lifetime. I will be looking straight ahead for a while, as though I had not heard, and then, in a surprisingly loud and angry voice, I will answer — to the room, to the young man, to the world: "Not . . . a . . . god . . . damn . . . thing."

HYMNS DO NOT speak any louder to worshippers in church than juke box music does to young people waiting in the bus station cafe.

They sit at their tables, looking past coffee cups, wadded napkins, cigarette ashes, and they listen. They are being Spoken To. They listen to "Hey, Jude" and "Bridge Over Troubled Water" and an All-Feeling Sound wraps them together, warming them, telling them they are not alone. The music reassures them in their nighttime solitariness. They are deeply in it, as in God.

HOW CURIOUS: I now have a Name in the state. Not much of one, to be sure, but a name known by a handful of the knowledgeable few. I am now Someone-to-Watch. Yet, ironically, I am probably *through*. I am going to be another one who did not Fulfill His Promise.

EACH DAY WE SHOULD be able to say Thank You for life. We should make a religion — if that is the word — out of experiencing the world. We do not need churches or rituals or threats-of-sinfulness inherited from the past. We need eyes to see and ears to hear. We need only to be awed, daily.

HAD THERE BEEN only mornings available, I would have probably become someone else. But because of afternoons, I became me.

I WISH TO GOD I could put down in words the momentousness of our being.

I SIT DOWN at the typewriter and immediately become impatient — hostile to the idea of shaping words. I am no longer the sad lover embracing, in secret, the amours of his imagination.
Maybe that is part of it too. That I am not deeply sad any more — and, lacking such delicious sadness, cannot enter poetically into life. Or maybe I don't love very much any more — at least things of the past: Perhaps the past has, for whatever reasons, finally sighed and lay down and *become* past.

I DON'T NEED A TRIP to Acapulco: In my own backyard I

have blazing sun, rich white walls, pink oleanders, blue sky beyond pomegranate trees. . . .

YOU READ THE great novelists early and don't go back to them. You reach your peak too soon and then, in unconscious frustration, spend the following years vainly searching for that earlier sense of grandeur.

OUR LIVES: we are captive within them.

ONE AFTERNOON in the public relations department of El Paso Natural Gas, a nattily dressed young man sat with one ear pointed deferentially in the direction of the conference leader while he surreptitiously gazed at eye matter on the end of his moist finger. He gazed intently at it for some little time and then, after disposing of it in a careful flicking liaison between his fingers and his chair, he turned — rather sadly, I thought — back to the pressing business at hand.

I STARTED BACK toward the center of town, taking my time, looking at chinaberry trees, sleeping dogs, buses lumbering through the narrow streets. But mainly I found myself looking at faces, the faces of the poor: the constantly, extravagantly, unending poor of the back streets of Juarez.
My feet hurt but I kept on walking. By the time I came to the market district I was drunk on old cars and old clothes, on worn-down bodies and faces — drunk on the wine of poverty. I stopped beneath the roof of a melon stand, among the people, saying to myself, dazed: The human spectacle is too intense; I cannot bear it.

BYRON: I love him, too. He came along, and for a while I was not sure what my feelings toward him would be. Could I touch him gladly the way I touched Deborah? Could I respond deeply, completely?

I wondered, and changed his diapers, and watched him grow.

. . . Hug him, the way I had his sister? Delight in his smooth flesh, be charmed by his ways?

Yes.

ART (writing) must never be subsidized because it is nothing unless it is an act of survival — an expression of a self as it reacts to the deep pressures of living.

THERE ARE TIMES in teaching when I give all of myself, I do not hold back, I put intensity into English II.

But when the classroom hour is through a deep depression comes over me, and a feeling close to bitterness.

You see, I give all that I have to give: I clown, I question, I deliver the truths of my own living, I listen to the other voices I encourage to speak — and perhaps it is all for nothing.

. . . Thus, there is a sense of despair born out of expectation, of commitment — and then, ultimately, out of a sense of uncertainty. Time moves on when the bell rings, and there is no record of the hour. Maybe there is no real significance to be found in my many words and in their many faces.

(I feel a sense of frustration in teaching that is different from the frustration in writing: In teaching, my passion is not translated into the formation of an object — a word, a page. It is spread out — lost, perhaps — in the lives of young people who smile and breathe and seem interested and then walk away to other places . . . 125 bodies and faces this year, 125 next — and always the memory of those 125 of each year past.

(It is like teaching a school of piranha fish that feed constantly on your emotions and leave you, finally, picked clean.)

WE HAVE a hard time coming to grips with *love*, the most difficult word in the language, mainly because it is capable of bringing us so much pleasure and pain.

We look favorably on love, but we are suspicious of it.

Someone else's love, to us, is mere foolishness, and we observe it indulgently. Our love, however, is always pure passion.

Since we know that love brings out our weaknesses — makes us vulnerable — we do not easily admit to love even when we feel it. We do not casually say, "I love this thing, or that person." Such a guileless declaration makes us open to attack from a world which, we feel, seldom rewards lovers. We never want to admit our loves until the last possible moment — when we are finally so caught up in them that we are willing to sacrifice anything we have for their sake.

Thus people who talk openly, readily, about love — who seem to feel comfortable using the word — are regarded by us as being a bit phony, or unmanly, or too easily swayed by sentimentality. We suspect anyone who does not hide his loves the way a quail hides its nest.

Who knows: perhaps we feel this way because most of us are not innocent enough — which may mean strong enough — to love. Perhaps we are corrupted and made weak by our guilts and fears and thus must conceal our real selves behind carefully arranged masks.

Love happens to the young because they are marvelously free and unemcumbered. They are able to respond with an absolute commitment of themselves to whatever or whomever they find pleasing. Love for adults is not any harder, of course; it is just that the opportunities to indulge in varied loves seem to be rarer. For love *is* an indulgence, a complete immersion of a person in his love object, and an adult has so many responsibilities, loyalties, considerations that, for him, simple and direct reaction becomes increasingly difficult.

Love cannot flourish within a framework of complexity — since the other names for love are *directness, total-response, joy.* That is why many adults who begin to miss the pleasure of knowing love as they knew it when they were young — love of another person, love of fishing on a pleasant day, love of the sun on their bodies — rediscover it as parents, in reacting to the charms of their first-born. . . . Here, again, they discover, is the good embrace of flesh, the unqualified smile. The infant daughter or son can pull the father's hair, pinch his nose, beat small hands into his face — and to the father it is all sweetness and light.

Love is rare only because we cannot — or do not — make ourselves free enough to participate in it. As we grow older life makes us increasingly more thoughtful and concerned; it ties us to problems and routines; it hurts. And — as we look out from the world of our duties and constrictions — some of us even tend to become suspicious of love, of easy and spontaneous delights, while others of us simply become jealous. From our weary heights we gaze down on the Young Innocents and their loves and we say: "Why, they actually seem to be *enjoying* themselves.". . . We find this rather unfair (We're not enjoying *our*selves. . . .) and, indeed, if we could — under the guise of helping the young see the error of their ways — we would take them and their loves and break them apart. "It is for your own good," we would declare; "you will appreciate our wisdom when you reach a saner, steadier age."

Either that, or we would put love away in some safe, respectable place — in a great Museum of Human Values — so that we would not have to test it, personally, day by day. We could then choose certain trusted representatives who each year would go into the museum and check on Love, shining there under glass; and after picking up a small American flag to wave slowly these representatives would make their annual report to us in song: assuring us, the way Judy Garland used to do at the end of her nightclub act, that love was still the secret that made us, and our country, strong. And with our duty to honor an eternal human verity thus discharged, we would not have to think further about it. We would not let it bother us in the performance of our daily lives.

I DISTRUST — dislike, I suppose — all purists, idealists, overly righteous reformers. They are anti-human even when they are most fervently humanistic. They never quite seem to learn that every virtue hides its own particular evil.

THE PAST IS so much past it always seems like a lie. . . . I *was*, in so many places and I *am*, so differently now.
. . . Time, the subtle magician that distorts reality. Rather: there *is* no reality simply because there is time.

WHEN ROUTINES of work are done and I am driving slowly home, I think again that one unforgettable thought which has been waiting for me all during the day: the thought of death that slams through me like the quick surge of an electric current and makes me almost recoil physically against the back of the car seat. I continue to gaze ahead through the windshield, looking for all the world like any other home-bound, five o'clock driver, yet I am sunk into depression, paralyzed by the awareness that all my daily concerns add up to nothing. I turn familiar corners, getting closer to home, and all I can think of is: All in vain, All in vain. . . .

I AM WAITING at a red light on South El Paso Street as I stroll about town. It is a Saturday evening in December about six o'clock and there are a lot of people on the move, a lot of neon flashing in front of stores, a lot of cars passing by.

As I wait I hear snatches of conversation, the beginnings of arguments, loud laughter. Mexican men who have spent the afternoon in bars are out on the sidewalk, blinking uncertainly, their beer-reddened faces solemn and subdued. Soldiers are walking by in two's and three's on their way to Juarez. Short plump Mexican girls with elaborate hairdos and tight-fitting black dresses clatter up from basement dance halls in their high heels and rush around the corner to sidewalk telephones.

It is a typical Saturday-night moment, with people doing what people generally do on South El Paso Street.

. . . As I stand there I happen to look west where there is still a last wide glow on the horizon and a single thin cloud floating above the top of a warehouse.

Just a red glow before complete darkness, one last suggestion of a cloud.

And suddenly, there I am again with an old familiar thought jabbing at my mind: Humans, busy on the earth, occupied with their personal affairs, and not seeing — or caring about — that western horizon of their lives, that dim glow in the west that always means things not *of* their earth: that means blackness, eternity, mystery, infinite space.

IN THIS HIGH SCHOOL there are people. They come from homes and families, and they have lungs and intestines and arteries and minds. They walk the halls each day, and at certain hours they place themselves in special rooms that are called classes. In these classes they listen to other people, called teachers. They answer questions at the end of chapters, and when the bell rings they move through the doorway into the hall outside. Perhaps they say words to friends in passing, perhaps not; then, in a few minutes, they enter another classroom and sit once more in chairs, one body placed behind another.

Sad to say, they do this for five days a week, four weeks out of a month, nine months each year. And since they are regarded as a special category of people they have a special kind of name; they are called Students. To many teachers, this name does not suggest that they possess any of the dreams and fears and needs and preoccupations that other humans have; indeed, the name Student tends to imply that they are not significantly humans at all.

"LIFE IS HOLY." That is said every so often, and I believe it. I do not give a damn how anyone cares to interpret it religiously — within the framework of traditional religions. I simply know that there is no other summarizing remark that is as true.

I EXPERIENCED, for a moment, the Middle Ages.

I was standing at the edge of San Elizario, at dusk, when the bell of the Catholic church began to sound.

The sun was far past the horizon and the branches of the many bare December trees were spread out finely against a pale afterglow in the west. Water ran nearby in a canal and cold air was moving along the ground. Crickets had started in the ditches. Boys were yelling in the distance, calves were bawling, dogs barked. Lanterns were giving faint glows from adobe houses half-sunk into the growing darkness. There were brief, idle rattlings — buckets and doors.

As the dogs kept barking and the leafless trees grew dimmer in the orange strip of the leftover sky, I had the feeling that the earth was large and men were small, that simple ways of working and living were the best, that it was good to stay in the presence of animals and the land.

I stood there, with the finality of night just moments away. The cold increased and the trees gradually disappeared and the bell clanged rhythmically across the fields.

AT 39 I AM A LOVER who has asked too many times that life declare its intentions. I have never received a reply, of course, yet like all Old Beaus, I stick around, available, just in case. . . .

WORDS CHEAPEN EXPERIENCE. We assume that since we make use of a word which describes or stands for a thing, then we are actually coming to grips with the thing itself. In having available such words as *miracle, holy, awesome, profound,* we believe that the mouthing of them somehow makes us participate in some act other than mere speech. Thus we never really try to enter deeply into experiences which words stand for. We dismiss miracles from our minds simply by calling them that: miracles.

To see . . . is astonishing; to think . . . is fantastic. Yet even to use such words—*astonishing, fantastic*—is to stop trying to grasp the essential nature of seeing and thinking. Words, in becoming such easy substitutes for the thing-in-itself, have gradually robbed life of its (glory) and (awe) and (power) . . . Name it, and it dies for us. . . . Yet apparently, the urge of civilized man is to do exactly that: to name, to categorize: to attempt to master life through a continual verbalization of things in it: to reduce its mystery by giving mystery various labels.

To name does not explain, and long after we have said, "I am," we still do not know what we have said.

OVER THERE, across the border in El Paso, my house is sleeping. John, the white cat, is sitting in the kitchen window, waiting my return. The rabbit is sprawled out beside the garden; the ducks have buried heads under their wings.

Here, in Juarez, in the old city market, men in coats and turned-down caps stand in doorways, watching the deserted stalls. It is cold. The men are surrounded by looming shapes, by the sense of we-are-all-in-this-business-together—the business of poverty, which is not just a word here but a way of life. It *is* life, like the darkness and the cold. . . .

HAVEN'T YOU EVER touched a sleeping child — your own — and then stood looking at her body curved into itself in rest? Haven't you wondered not only where her mind was at that moment but how it was possible that such a walking, speaking, *reacting* child could turn, within minutes, into a body and nothing more (quite peaceful looking, yes, and apparently free from any pain, but nevertheless in a corpse-like state: a passive figure unable during her time of sleep to do any of that walking and speaking and reacting which characterized her as a vital, unique personality)?

I repeat, haven't you ever done this kind of wondering while looking down at your child — so close there on the bed yet, for the time of her sleep, totally beyond ordinary communication? . . .

Well, I have, and to do so is to call forth the whole stunning mystery of life and death. I have stood there knowing that on some future day someone else will be looking in at her in some quiet room, and apparently she will once again merely be lying tranquilly asleep. Yet in fact she will be dead. And the unanswerable question of today will be the same stark unanswerable question then: What in the name of God and man is a mind, a brain, a personality? Where does it live and how does it die? How does it differ from that flesh and blood which it inhabits? What is a human being; what is a human being's body?

THERE IS A pleasing kind of woman's mouth that swings open easily, rather widely, and is filled with handsome white teeth. . . . A lovely kind of mouth, very friendly and generous, and when it smiles it seems to be saying: Look at me, enjoy me, come inside me, even, for I am always open — my mouth and body and I — to you and the world.

One young woman with such a mouth looks like a supremely intelligent goat. When her lips spread back to show the clean, good-looking teeth — and the lower lip becomes a sensitive red pouch of flesh — she becomes goat, Charlie Chaplin, female satyr: all in one.

IT HAS JUST struck me that before too long my children will be passing beyond their present states of pleasant ignorance and will be entering that long miserable stretch in which they confront life in all its pain.

What will I be able to do for them? Can I do more for Deborah and Byron than my own parents were able to do for me? They loved me, but they were of no help as I floundered to get past all the sharp edges of reality.

. . . Here I have been — just trying to survive and finally having managed to reach a somewhat acceptable ledge above all my personal chasms — yet as I turn around to view my position I see those two small figures headed out of my house and down the trail toward Experience — clothed, as I was, as all people are, in gigantic ignorance.

THE PAST CAN ONLY be reached now by art, not by visits home.

COLLEGE GIRLS at the Bar Central:
Slight bodies under straight blond hair; dresses like colored napkins placed neatly on the bodies of dolls.
Girls aware of themselves, smiling toward one another as their fingers keep touching hair back from their eyes.
Girls standing with drinks in their hand, faces ready to turn toward their college-boy dates, who are rolling dice in leather cups.
Girls with straight-falling hair and ice-filled drinks and lightly covered bodies: at the bar: waiting.

A YOUNG MEXICAN GIRL walks home with her mother. The girl, holding books against her breast, is trim and neat. The mother is bulky-looking in her old black coat and scarf; she hobbles along, leaning to one side, walking without gracefulness. The two of them pause at the Barrel House corner, waiting for the light to change so they can cross to the plaza.
The girl has been to the library to study after school; the mother is getting off work from her job as a cleaning woman. And now they are walking along together: the daughter light-footed, Anglicized, perhaps college-bound; the mother slow-gaited, stolid, tired: a Mexican-woman-from-the-South-Side.

I AM NO LONGER hunting for truths now and therefore I no longer hurt very strongly, no longer feel so puzzled, anguished, full of despair. I am, you see, in my late thirties, and paying for it. I have finally established routines of living that satisfy; I have gained a certain harmony in my life. I am no longer driven — and I simply do not know what to do about it. With old urgencies gone, I am completely out of gear. I believe in nothing, really —

neither progress, art, nor beauty. I am a private investigator of the world who, suddenly, has nothing to investigate. There are still a thousand causes to embrace — if I wanted causes; there are still a thousand places to see — if I wanted escape. But there is only one me, and unless I can say, This I Want, or This I Believe — and mean it — then I will stay without a cause and will have no real place to go.

WE MUST REMEMBER that there was, indeed, a ninth century and that it was fully a hundred years long: that people lived, day by day, in 836, in 837, in 838, and looked forward perhaps to 839 in hopes that it might bring a change of fortune. . . . A man in 838 would finish his midday meal, belch, scratch a scab on his arm, and wonder about those things which men wondered about in 838. He was a man like any man anytime: caught up in daily routines, unsure of tomorrow, surrounded by the mysteries of living.

. . . We accept so much intellectually. Why, yes, of course, we say, men lived in the ninth century — but we fail to be humbled or amazed at such a fact because we do not really feel the words as we say them. We do not react to knowledge imaginatively. And yet it is only through imaginative perception that we ever change mere facts into understandings.

THE TWO WORST conditions of life are these: 1. having no personal freedom, and 2. having absolute personal freedom.

A COMMUNITY of quiet lives exists outside my back door:
Night comes, there is a chill in the air, and I stand in the presence of our backyard animals. The rabbit, the cats, the dog, the ducks, the chicken, the quail — they are licking fur, scratching feathers, lying motionless and content. I stand among them, in the dark, pleased by their animal sanity.

NOBODY KNOWS ME; I'm not sure what would happen if anyone ever did.

SHORT OF WRITING letters to God, and hoping they get there: what to do?

NATURE LEADS ME gently, by the hand, into a brick wall.

FOR AN ADULT, life is one-half living and one-half *awareness* of living. It is not just walking down the sidewalk: it is being aware of the walking.

Living finally takes on double dimensions; reality shifts its ground. An event is no longer an event, as it used to be in childhood. It is an event-plus, an event-as-perceived-by-humans.

This double-vision comes and goes. For a while we can eat a popsicle, paint a board, talk with a friend, and we see only the solid outline of the event itself. Then, without warning, we see our feet walking along or hear our son's voice and it is as if we were watching a movie: they are both real and unreal, that foot, that voice. They exist . . . *over there*, in a strange vacuum of a separate time and a separate space. They are unconnected to us. They are suddenly pure phenomena, beyond human control or comprehension.

I SAW THE pleasing profile of a girl; I saw the shape of her face, turned sideways.

She was in class, listening to a record I was playing, and she was turned a bit in her desk, looking toward the windows. She was a straight-D student, limp, disinterested; brown hair parted in the middle and stringy; no make-up; child of divorced parents.

Yet as I looked at her, turned in her desk, she was suddenly someone special. There was in her profile the outline of a human personality — no, more than that: the outline of all human personality. Suddenly, listening to George Harrison's "My Sweet Lord," she became a quietly pretty girl, a thoughtful girl, she was Potential and Sensitivity and Feeling and the History of the Race. She was not just another face-among-faces: she was everything we have been living throughout history for; she was the end product of several billion years of evolution. In that split moment when she turned in her chair and gazed toward the window she was more than herself: she became immortalized, my own sixth-period Mona Lisa.

PERHAPS LIFE IS a mere tantalizing. We are separated briefly from God in order that we may feel, for a while, what it is like not to *be* God.. Perhaps all human feeling, all sensibility, is just an awareness of alienation.

I COULD NOT have continued to write and file away, write and file away, unless I felt that I was somehow enlisted in the cause of truth — that even if what I wrote was never published it would nevertheless be *down*, it would be *said*.

I guess it was my belief that "someday" what I had thought and written would be valued, and that simply trying to be honest as I went along — though unpublished — would have to be reward enough. (For no entirely selfish motive — lust for influence or fame — could have possibly been strong enough to keep me writing during the long uninterrupted days of complete obscurity. If I could not have felt a sense of worthy participation in the discovery of truth I would have had to shove pencil and paper aside in despair and try to find some other way to make my personal scratch on the walls of the universe.)

I'VE HAD MY LITTLE SAY and now I guess it is time to quit.

I was in pain for a number of years and I found that writing down words about my state of pain brought — if not the answers I wanted — at least a bit of relief and a vague sense of accomplishment.

Finally, at 39, I am at a place in my life where only my family and my teaching job are the concerns of my days. The old writing urge that sustained me in earlier years of loneliness is gone.

Perhaps if I say it once and for all, aloud, to the air — voice the acceptance of what has changed rather than merely think about it, brood about it — I will be freed to build toward some kind of second life.

. . . Therefore, to this May afternoon, I speak these words as a death sentence to that part of me which was once so vitally alive: "My writing days are over, and I am sorry they are gone. I wish they could have stayed with me longer for they were the greatest company I have ever known. I do not know what I will do now in my deep-mood times, since I have no other resources to combat the aloneness of being alive — to occupy the passions of my deepest self. As I step into my fortieth year I am without answers and — even worse — without questions. I merely am: alive, in part."

I LOOK AROUND and see that the world is supreme and I am nothing. I continue to be intimidated by life, by all that I see and feel. It is a case of trembling before Creation.

TRUTHS HAVE NO meaning unless we are living them.

ALWAYS, IN THE SUMMERTIME, when I am released from the routines of teaching and have time on my hands, when I sink into myself again — always when I turn myself over to the rhythms of nature and the universe, I think of death. I focus deeply on non-human purposes and things. Like a piece of wood gradually dislodged from shore by the slow working of the tide, I am floated outward . . . I drift among the weeds, the breezes, the gradual turning of morning into noon into evening into night. I become a piece of paper blowing across a cottonfield, a flower wobbling along a fence, a bird passing.

TO WRITE AGAIN: to be released back to myself, to woes and gnashings, to moans and smiles and tears; to quit this paralyzed place. To be able to feel a thing strongly and then write it down, to make a meaningful imprint on myself on paper. I have no work to do, no sense of engagement. There is no singing and no mourning in my life. I pass the days — level-eyed and barely breathing.

I vote for trees to take over the world. They are kings of the earth.

I have backed away from intelligence and have come to embrace a kind of divine idiocy. Human intelligence, I mean. Intelligence that prides itself on mastery of facts. Intelligence-test intelligence. Computer intelligence.

I identify with weeds and sun and ground. I give up thinking.

I am content to sit beside the chicken house and blend into the morning: to be as a post is, as grass is.

I look out at the radiant earth and I want to ask: Who is in charge of this production? . . . Why, that is a beautifully placed clump of Johnson grass over there; and that mountain range is elegant.

I am in this June day, on this plot of ground, the way my foot is in my shoe. I inhabit myself comfortably. I am friends with myself, with the water from the yard hydrant, with the passing hours.

I am here now behind my red plank fence, under the elm trees, with my family and animals. The mountains are nicely in the distance, and the cotton fields are nicely close. The house and yards have a rural air, although we are just ten minutes from town. . . . 425 Sunset Road is the address. It is where I live at age forty, in my newly bought old house.

I still have a job — I teach in a public high school — but I no longer have a calling, a goal in life. An inner platform has collapsed — the one on which the writer-image of myself rested as it tried to make special combinations of words. This platform was the only one I ever learned how to build. I built it, secretly, painfully, in my 20s and used it for ten years or so; then it began to disintegrate, settle in a slow-motion collapse. . . . A writer's platform, a private look-out tower where I sat inside myself, scouting the horizons for God, Meaning, Truth: it rotted away, leaving me hollow.

So I am here at the edge of town, feeding glossy red roosters and looking across cotton fields and smiling amiably at friends who occasionally drop by. I am lost but I do not cry out. Not yet. I fix a sagging gate and push my son in his swing and listen to the turkeys pecking at an empty pie pan. I walk around within my pleasant red fence and pick up candy wrappers and gaze out toward the freight train passing along the sand hills in the west. I throw grain to the ducks and keep myself under control, as I have always tried to do. The platform is gone — but then perhaps it was not everything. I am still all right with my trees and family and cotton fields. I am not desperate. Not yet.

Designed by

Evan Haywood Antone

```
R0154393625   TXR   T818
                     8666
       8.00


BODE, ELROY
       ALONE IN THE WORLD
LOOKING
```